FOR ALL TIMES

A 30 Day Morning & Evening Devotional

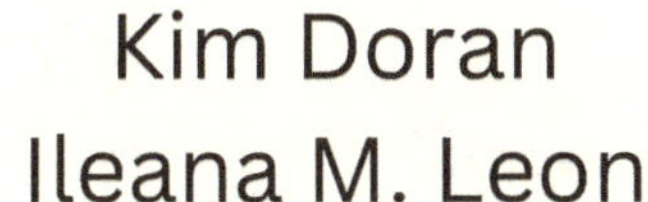

Kim Doran
Ileana M. Leon

First published by Kim Doran – Ileana M. Leon 2026
Anchor & Root Publishing

ISBN #978-1-737-1563-2-1

Cover by Canva
Scripture taken from the Holy Bible, NIV, NLT, ESV

Printed in the United States of America

Introduction

In the rhythm of our days, there are two sacred moments that quietly shape everything in between... when we first open our eyes in the morning, and when we lay our heads down at night.

Scripture calls us to anchor both: "When you lie down and when you rise up" (Deuteronomy 6:7), reminding us that God's Word is not just something we visit occasionally, but something meant to dwell with us, framing our beginnings and gently closing our days.

This 30-day devotional was created with that rhythm in mind. Each day offers both a morning and an evening reflection, inviting you to start your day centered in truth and end it wrapped in grace. What makes this journey especially meaningful is the shared voice behind it. Two women, two perspectives, one faithful God... woven together as they alternate writing each devotion. Their voices may differ, but their heartbeat is the same: to point you toward Him.

As you move through these pages, you'll notice something refreshing and deeply personal. These aren't distant or formal reflections; they read like conversations. Like sitting across the table from a trusted friend over coffee, hearing real stories, honest struggles, and faith-filled insights that meet you right where you are.

Whether you come to these pages full of faith or simply longing for more, my hope is that this devotional becomes a steady companion guiding your thoughts in the morning, settling your heart at night, and reminding you that God is present in every moment in between.

Gena B. McCown
Author, Speaker, Ministry Leader

Gena B. McCown is the author of Women's Ministry with Purpose, Still Here & Still Struggling to Lead, and the Into the Deep Series of Devotional Journals. A South Florida native and ministry leader of over thirty years in the church and within the community.

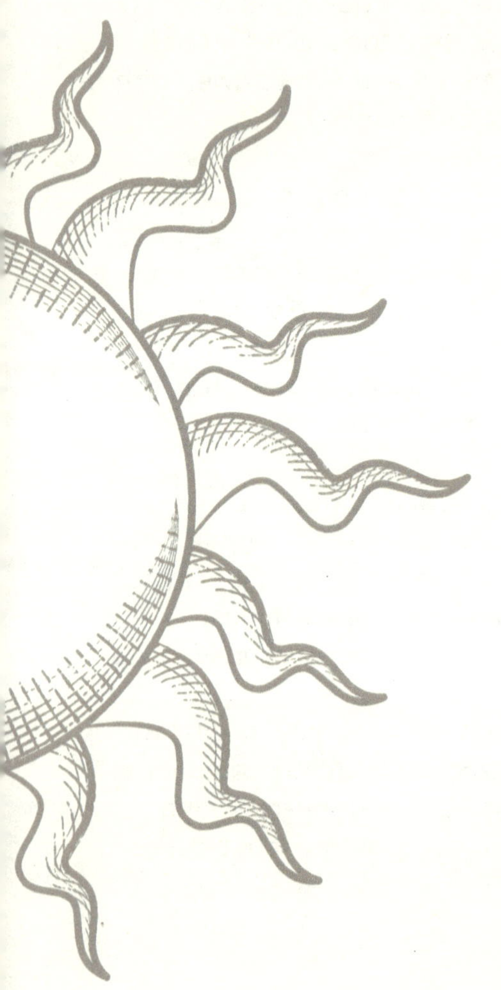

REBIRTH

Open wide the windows
Let sunlight pour in
No more darkened shadows
Thoughts whirl and spin

The sleepiness shaken
Birds' melodies sing
The sizzle of bacon
Cell buzzes and pings

Coffee is brewing
Pressing message heard
The mind needs renewing
Our refuge, His Word

Sipping and reading
Heart has received
With guidance and leading
Will not be deceived

Sweet peace overflowing
Thoughtful crafted reply
Hurt and conflict resolving
Ending all sinful pride

Sould freed, unshackled
Potter molding clay
Guilt and shame tackled
Releasing all pressing weight

Lips shouting in thankful praise
Joy bursting from every pore
The Creator's perfect love relayed
Ready to face the day once more

Author Ileana M. Leon

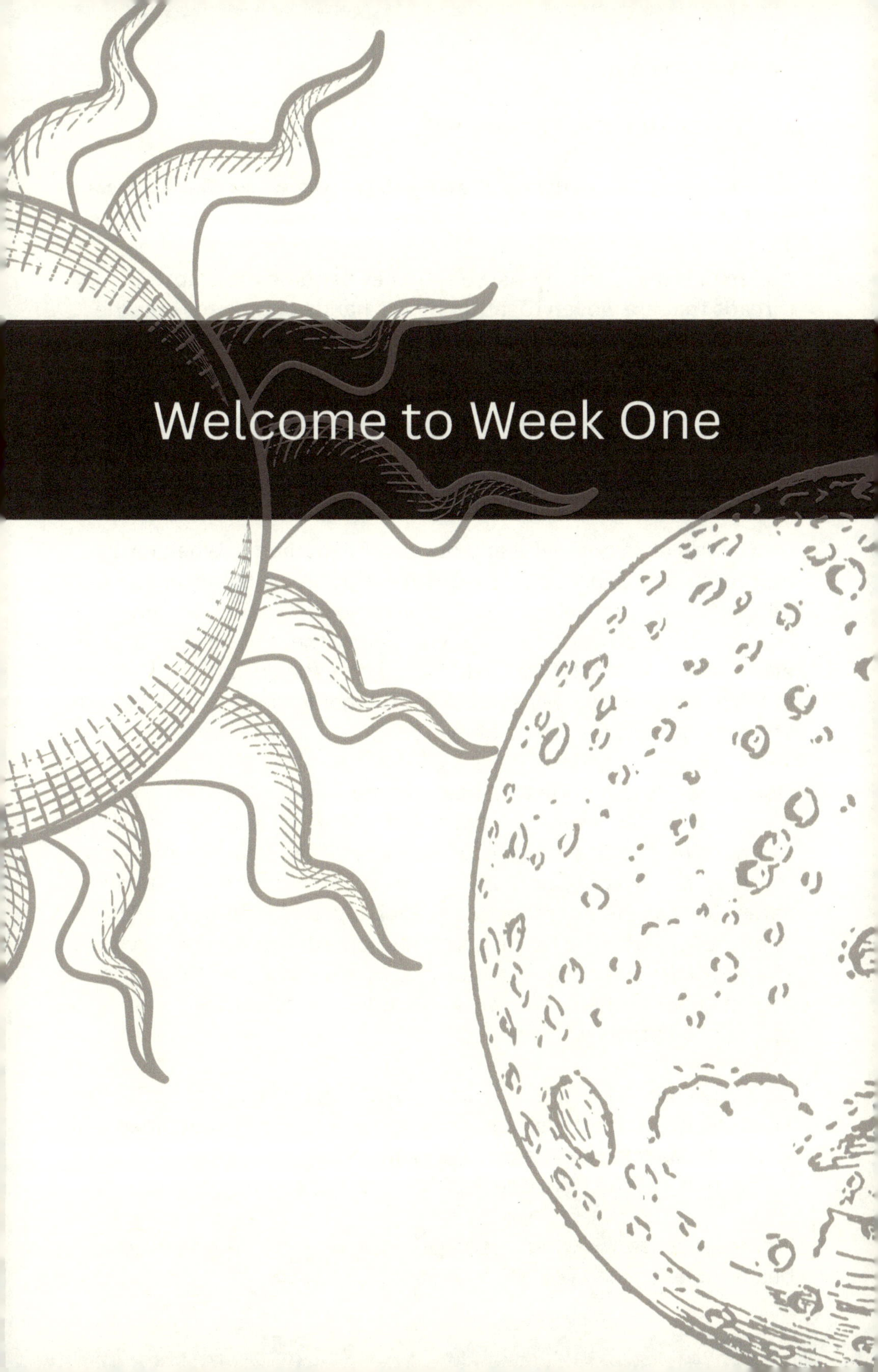

Welcome to Week One

Day 1...Morning

MEMORIES THAT SHAPE OUR LIVES

He has made everything beautiful in his time. Ecclesiastes 3:11

Ah... memories...so many. As we age, they become the colorful threads that are woven together by the hands of time to form the unforgettable, priceless tapestry that shapes our lives. Interlaced are the snapshots of family, friends, and unique experiences. The golden fibers of laughter, dark grey lines of pain, and the ruby-red ribbons of love and joy all come together to form our story. Whether good or bad, they are gifts that grow more precious with each passing year.

God is with us in our joyful and our painful moments. When my firstborn was diagnosed with Autism and Tourette Syndrome, my life felt as if it was unraveling. Yet God never left me alone. Looking back, I can see through every medical visit, every therapy session, and every sleepless night, I was held by the crimson cord of His grace and love. My son is a gift, teaching me daily to knit faith and courage into the fabric of my life.

One golden recollection that has become a treasured memory is the day my daughter, after a painful divorce, married the man who truly saw her. The one God had set apart for her. That day, we witnessed my daughter live out Joel 2:25. God restored what the locust had eaten. To hear their personal vows exchanged against the backdrop of praise and worship to the Lord, was something out of a fairy tale. The song that was sung, The Blessing, by Kari Jobe and Cody Carnes, became their anthem. This was the answer to my earnest, desperate, tear-soaked prayers.

Memories remind us not only where we have been, but how God has faithfully walked with us. Some of your tapestry may be stained with your tears as mine has been. That is okay; they add to the authenticity of the weave revealing our strength and courage.

Whatever season you are in, trust that He is weaving something beautiful, even if all you see are loose threads.

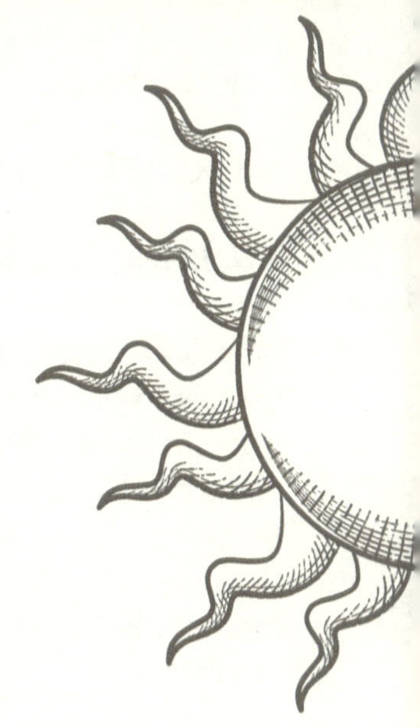

REFLECTION:

Day 1...Evening

MEMORIES THAT SHAPE OUR LIVES

All things are possible with God. Mark 10:27

Memories, there are so many acquired throughout the years. Etched in our minds and swelling up our hearts. Some good, some not, yet they bring emotions to the surface. From laughter that spills out without warning causing a contagious reaction on others. Or, tears, simple and wet streaming down cheeks and landing where they may. These experiences help form who we are for each memory is either bitter or sweet. But rest assured, it is as it is meant to be.

Up until this point in my life, the memory that takes center stage for me is the day my daughter entered the world. Something I doubted would happen became reality and my life changed forever. All that time trying with the disappointing news of negative results. All the prayers left unanswered. The discouragement felt after hearing I may never have a child of my own tore my heart apart in a thousand shattered pieces. But, those emotions, those moments of hurt were now replaced with the living, breathing, heartbeat of a baby. My child. Her eyes open wide, shining and searching for the voice she had heard over the months in the womb.

God heard and God answered. Not in my timing, but in His. When I threw in the towel, ran my mouth and focused on another direction He made what I thought impossible, so very possible. This incredible experience of becoming a mother has shaped every single day I have walked through. Laughter and tears joined forces, and my doubt was completely washed away. The physical and emotional pain long forgotten as sheer joy beyond my understanding became relevant.

The beauty of creation, reflection of childbirth, and precious new life are the very core that shape mankind. Life certainly changes and allows a multitude of memories to be made and shared throughout the years. Our God can do all things, not just for me, but for you as well. So, wherever you are today, I hope your prayers get answered. As you look back over your life memories, may you see more sweet than bitter.

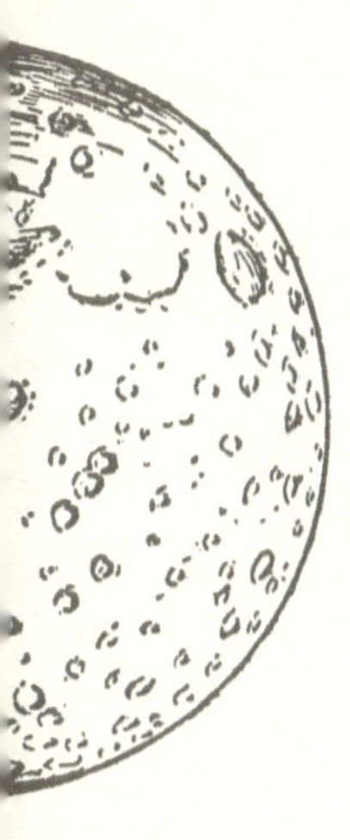

REFLECTION:

Day 2...Morning

WORDS FROM THE HEART

"Whoever has ears to hear, let them hear." Mark 4:9

There are so many people I hold dear to my heart, even if I do not see them often. Some I see too much and may take that for granted. Although, each one leaves a mark upon me.

Reflecting on friendships and tough times brings to my mind one person who stands out for her words from the heart. She absolutely got my attention. A thirty-year friendship of special moments, holidays, vacations, and raising our children. A sister, not by blood, but by bond. In her gentle way I was told, "You need God!"

See, on the surface I was all put together, a great career, family and all the material things. However, inside I was a mess. I did not speak it, but she knew. Her own life was filled with heartache. I tried to support her while struggling with my own life choices. But that's what friends are for, in good times and in bad.

During one of our talks, she mentioned being back in church for comfort, community, and a fresh start. Her marriage was in the process of divorce. Many voices, meaning well, gave her advice, yet she turned to God. Sincere admiration for her strength and ability to forgive her husband. She wanted to honor her vows despite feeling alone, confused, angry, and judged. We shared these feelings, different circumstances, nonetheless, same emotions.

She waited on God to answer. While I continued to live with secrets and lies. Until she called me out! It trul y surprised me, hitting me right where I needed it most. Wearily, I accepted her church invitation. Once inside, worship started and my walls came tumbling down like Jericho. Tears spilled out, my legs buckled, and I fell into my seat. Each word of each song hit me. My friend held my hand as my daughter hugged me. The cleansing came that night as I surrendered everything to God. For such a time as this!

With God all things are possible. Do you need to hear or share some heartfelt words? Maybe your words could help save a life.

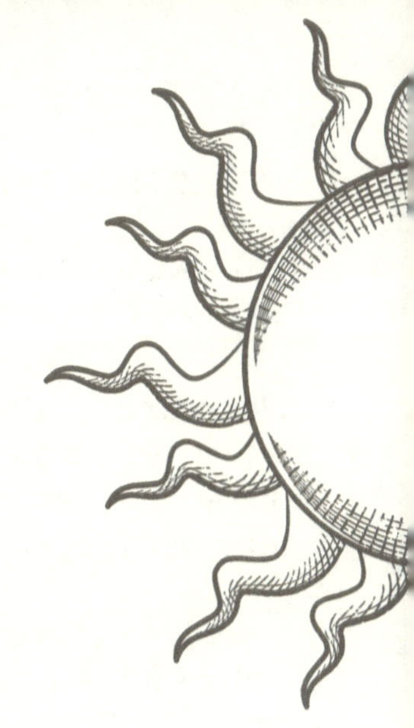

REFLECTION:

Day 2...Evening

WORDS FROM THE HEART

The tongue has the power of life and death, and those who love it will eat its fruit. Proverbs 18:21

We speak a lot, don't we? Words tumble out of our mouth and sometimes we don't even realize what we are saying. Words have power. They can inflict damage to our hearts and minds that can last for years. They can also be used to heal and repair old wounds.

The Bible states that the power of life and death is in the tongue. But it also says as a man thinks, he is. Those are two things that go hand and hand. We must be mindful of how we relate to others, but what about how we talk to ourselves? That constant chatter in our heads needs to be uplifting and productive. If we are honest, it seldom is.

Humans spend a lot of time and money making sure they take care of their bodies, but did you know that self-care includes our minds as well? It is not acceptable to constantly be belittling ourselves. If a friend makes a mistake, we encourage them so they can fix the problem. We season our speech with salt and light. Salt preserves truth and light dispel darkness. On the other hand, if it's us who failed, we beat ourselves up for days. No wonder we carry so much anxiety and stress. We are our own worst enemy. It is time to stop this cycle of personal abuse.

To end the unhelpful self-talk, it is imperative we use a trusted source to battle our inner dialogue. I can't think of a better source than God's Word. Let me ask you, what do you think God says about you? I can guarantee it is not what you tell yourself in frustrating times.

God tells us in Psalm 139:14 That all of us are fearfully and wonderfully made. God does not make junk. In Romans 5:8 He tells us that we are valuable enough to die for. There is scripture after scripture that says how important we are to the Creator of the Universe. If you want to change the narrative you tell yourself, I invite you to pick up the Bible and start speaking into your soul. It is His language of undeniable love.

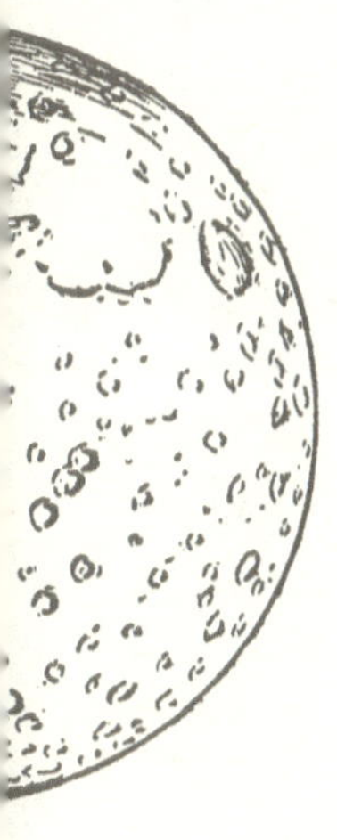

REFLECTION:

Day 3...Morning

WISDOM FOR THE AGES

Listen to advice and accept discipline, and in the end, you will be counted among the wise. Proverbs 19:20

Many years ago, I was at a crossroad in life going through the daily motions with no clear direction. I remember being on the phone with my father, who resided on the west coast with a three-hour time difference. We talked once or twice a week.

Simply adored these calls as it made the miles feel not so distant. My dad was more of a talker; however, he also listened. I guess that is where I get it from. At one such time, we talked about my current job status. I loved working at a private club as a bartender. It had great hours, a beautiful view, fabulous food, and a diverse population. Yet I knew this was not meant to be long term. I was seeking but did not know what.

Dad, aka Jimmy Mc, in wisdom and love, offered me an opportunity I declined many times before, to go to college. In my younger years, I thought it was not necessary. But truthfully, a longing developed to grow in knowledge and opportunities. So, I accepted graciously. The process was intimidating, yet soon that was replaced with excitement. My work schedule got shorter to make room for school. My father blessed me greatly and enabled me to focus on my education.

One thing he spoke carries me through my life, "No matter what you choose to be in life, be kind and be educated. It will open a whole new world for you." Such a wise and giving man he was. I took his advice and got the four-year degree in Criminal Justice/Psychology. Doors indeed did open. Advice is not my thing, but rather give suggestions, and looking back I see that is exactly what my dad did. He presented some roads and gave me the chance to choose.

Now I offer a suggestion to you, first and foremost pray. Let God direct to who and when. Be quick to listen, slow to speak. Then pray again on what you learned. A new direction you will find. How do I know this? Well, let's say practice gave me the wisdom I gained.

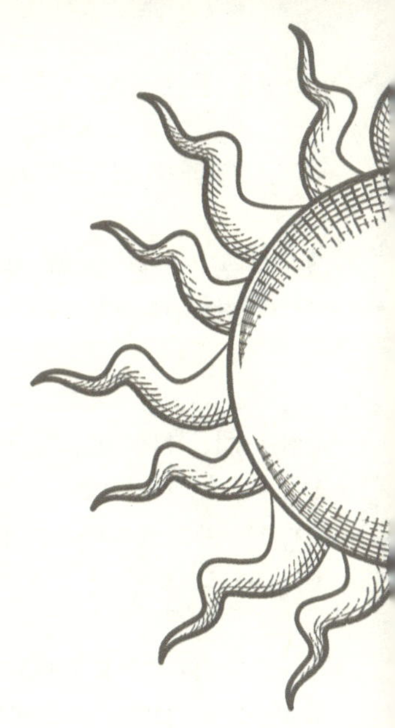

REFLECTION:

Day 3...Evening

WISDOM FOR THE AGES

Set a guard over my mouth, Lord; keep watch over the door of my lips. Psalm 141:1-3

"Shut your mouth!" That was the advice given to me by a ninety-year-old. Normally, such vocabulary might have offended me. But this elderly gentleman was not being rude or mean-spirited. He was my friend, a man of integrity and strong faith; someone I highly respected.

This surprising guidance came immediately after he had prayed a powerful prayer over me. At the time, I couldn't understand why this usually soft-spoken grandfather did not explain his harsh-sounding directive. Yet, the way he looked at me, with his soulful eyes, was evident that he would not add anything further. His advice lingered in my mind. Eventually, it faded, only to return in full force as a vital reminder during a heart-to-heart conversation with a family member.

One day, in prayer, I heard the same command again: "Shut your mouth." Then other words followed: "Let them be humans."

Placed together, these no longer served as stern corrections. "Shut your mouth, let them be human," was a heavenly instruction; a beacon of light guiding me through a family member's health crisis. It also served to help repair a fragile relationship. In those decisive moments when I had the urge to fight fire with fire, it settled my spirit. It taught me to zip it when I wanted to lash out and stay bitter.

Jesus didn't need to open His mouth to defend Himself. He knew when to speak and when to remain silent. Therefore, as His follower, I don't need to always have the last word, give unsolicited advice, or feel responsible for how others respond in conflict. This divine insight brought me peace and understanding in some very difficult situations. When well-intentioned counsel is not received kindly, it is better to stay quiet. Sometimes, the best answer lies in praying more and arguing less. I admit I am still learning to shut my mouth, but I am growing in the art of "letting them be humans."

REFLECTION:

Day 4...Morning

THE UNEXPECTED GIFT OF FRIENDSHIP

Oil and perfume make the heart glad, and the sweetness of a friend comes from his earnest counsel. Proverbs 27: 9

I have known my hairdresser for over 20 years. I found her during a trip to the mall with my mom, who was visiting from out of town and needed a cut. Having just moved to the area, I didn't know anyone personally. We opted for a small salon with light traffic.

Growing up with my mom's cousin as our beautician, taught us what to look for in a professional hairstylist. This expert hit all the marks. She was friendly, attentive, and skilled. After that positive experience, we trusted her to take care of the rest of the family. We were so pleased that we followed her even after she left for another location.

Through conversations and during hair appointments, I discovered how much we had in common. Our upbringing, our values, and our faith all aligned. After my mother passed, sitting in her chair became more than a part of my beauty routine, it was therapeutic.

Along with the flattering highlights and fashionable cuts, she offered pearls of wisdom that pierced through the dark veil of mourning. I always left not only looking better, but feeling comforted and understood. My turn came when she was hospitalized and I had the opportunity to help her rediscover her joy and lean on the strength God gave her.

Years have passed, and our relationship has grown from hair artisan to good friends. A trip to see her usually includes a deliciously homemade lunch, and in-depth conversation to catch up on our lives. She is also one of the most generous people I know. One visit I left her house with a bag full of fashionable dresses; some still had store tags on them.

Friendships can be born in the most unexpected places. All it takes is a smile and an open heart. You never know, someone may be searching for the very gift of friendship that lives inside you.

REFLECTION:

Day 4...Evening

THE UNEXPECTED GIFT OF FRIENDSHIP

How good and pleasant it is when God's people live together in unity! Psalm 133.1

This past year I spent my birthday on a cot in a hospital hallway. While waiting for a room to open and test results to come I voiced, "Happy Birthday to me, I'm alive!" Unknown to me, a group of friends were arriving at a local favorite place to celebrate. So much prep was made by a dear friend to surprise me, yet I was the one to give the surprise with my current demise. The phrase "party pooper" sounds about right. Thankfully, my mini time out was only a few days yielding nothing of serious concern. As well as my friends being gracious in understanding.

The following week, my friend, the party hostess, advised me of the surprise party gone south. She and another friend wanted to take me out for a quiet lunch. I was worn down honestly, but accepted, appreciating their kindness and effort to make my birthday special. I needed my girl time and then some sleep in that order.

A week after my official birth date I walked into that favorite place to meet my two friends. Instead, the tables were filled with familiar faces yelling "Surprise!" It was surreal, with flowers, food and balloons. It seemed as if the whole place knew I was coming. The clapping was epic.

I truly enjoyed being there but not being the center of attention. Feeling physically drained yet emotionally filled and so very grateful to be gifted with this special time. Recognizing that my friends showed up not once, but twice to celebrate with me. What can I say other than, "Happy Birthday to me, I'm alive!"

As they sang, I thanked God, for making the way. He is a friend that never leaves or forsakes. Know this, no matter where you are or what you walk through, He is there. A friend from the very beginning to the very end and beyond. We are better together.

REFLECTION:

Day 5...Morning

A TIME OF PEACE

May mercy, peace, and love be multiplied to you. Jude 1:2

It has taken me years, honestly been decades, to really know peace that surpasses understanding. Seems like there is always something that requires my full attention and often brings demands and of course stress. However, since overcoming a cancer battle that completely changed my life, I found inner calm. Yes, peace within. Sounds odd, doesn't it? But it's the truth and nothing but the truth.

Perhaps facing uncertainty and knowing time is not guaranteed has opened my eyes. Capturing moments that fill my world with priceless peace. The everyday list of things believed to be a must do now gets pushed aside. Instead taking in the precious moments of simplicity. Being still and know has become the forefront of each new day.

When I get the opportunity to share my poetry or to sing, I fall right into the incredible zone of bliss. Something happens internally that is hard to explain, yet it is so wonderful for my soul. If given the chance, that is a state of being I could put on repeat for every hour of my life.

Scripture shares that peace is what God gives all of us. Whether we choose to receive it and walk in it is the question. It may be hard to trust or even believe peace is possible, but it is. So many struggle through the days and nights when it does not have to be that way. Jesus walked as man to face the struggles because of His endless love for us. In John 14:27 He says, “Peace I leave with you; My peace I give to you.” So let those words be more than just words, let them touch your mind and heart.

REFLECTION:

Day 5...Evening

A TIME OF PEACE

I lift my eyes to the mountains, where does my help come from? My help comes from the Lord, the Maker of Heaven and earth.
Psalm 121:1

My mother's battle with cancer was an unexpected crisis. I don't have siblings and her passing meant the loss of my greatest confidant and support. There was not a day, we didn't speak to each other. No subject was too embarrassing or deep to discuss. She was my safe space. Her counsel always came from a place of love.

During her illness, I was led to read Psalm 121. Little did I know it would keep appearing, in songs, cards, and it would accompany me through waiting rooms and hospital stays. I never imagined that verse would also become my lifeline at her funeral.

Being an author, my comfort zone lies in expressing my feelings through my writing. Yet, the night before the funeral, I found myself unable to pen the eulogy. Since overwhelming heartache had robbed me of sleep, I opened my Bible to Psalm 121. Every word leaped off the page, reminding me I was not alone.

When I awoke the next day, the well of tears had run dry, and my mind was clear. That evening, when I stepped up to the microphone, I didn't feel any anxiety or grief. All my emotions that consumed me had been put on hold. I shared my treasured scripture, followed by an invitation to know Jesus, the one who sustained me. Looking back, I see the pause in my pain was necessary to accomplish the mission of sharing God's love with my father and all who mourned my mom.

Since then, I have seen that strength in a widow who still has words of thankfulness, or a mother who sings praises at her child's memorial. Only possible through the grace of God. Sometimes, that tranquility comes through His divine intervention. Other times, we must be willing to dig through the debris left to find it. Either way, He is with all of us in every storm. Do you want that kind of covering?

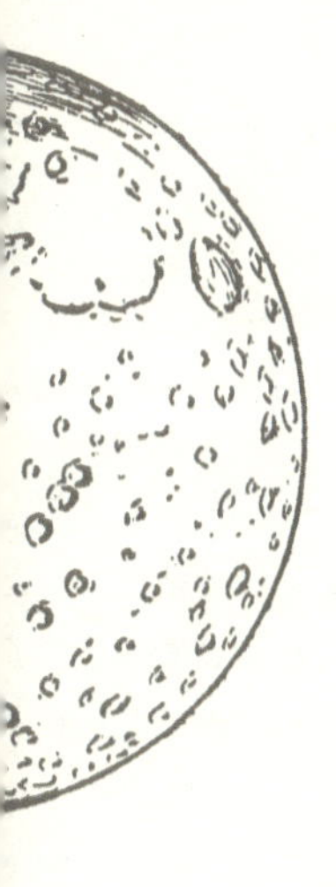

REFLECTION:

Day 6...Morning

WHEN MUSIC MOVES

Let us come before him with thanksgiving and extol him with music and song. Psalm 95:2

Music has the power to change a mood, shifting us from anxious and sad, to joyful and calm. In the 80's dancing was popular thing to do. My husband and I met dancing the night away at a night club. That thumping techno beat still carries so many memories of senior year and days at the beach.

Some songs pull at my heart strings. Like the song that we danced to on our wedding day, or songs passed down through my grandparents about my birthland. Others are songs that resonated with me because they remind me of a season I was searching for identity and meaning. Lyrics that built me up when life's problems seemed too much to handle. On a lighter note, there are silly songs that make us laugh. Those never grow old.

Today, I choose music that synchronizes my soul with my Heavenly Father. Something miraculous happens when we listen intently to anointed words set to music. They fill the heart with hope. At our lowest, this type of music can bring healing. It causes the soul to say goodbye to anxiety and hello to faith. These songs serve as a good reminder of His love and prepare us for earnest prayer and celebration.

Some have said my voice sounds like a "dying cow" when I sing. But you won't see me shy away from belting out praises to the One who gave me breath. Scripture tells us over 40 times to sing praises to the Lord. He longs to hear our voices lifted in worship.

My friend, whether you sing like an angel or a dying cow, sing loud and proud. Remember, God is not listening for the perfect pitch, but for a sincere, thankful heart.

REFLECTION:

Day 6...Evening

WHEN MUSIC MOVES

I will sing of your love and justice; to you, Lord, I will sing praise. Psalm 101:1

Oh, how I love music. As a vocalist, I recall amazing tunes that I have either heard or sung over the years. Hearing a melody flow and the emotions music brings to the surface are without measure.

My years have been adventurous. This city girl grew up on good old rock and roll. I indulged in the nightlife either as part of the band or to take in a good show. As I came to faith, I laid down that way and stepped into singing worship at church. From old to new so to say. From performance to praise and I've never looked back.

Music is universal and feeds an inner need. The catalog of songs available is mind blowing. Some I can name off the top of my head because of the impact made. "Joy in the Morning" by Tauren Wells, "there will be joy in the morning, joy in the morning, if it's not good, then He's not done, no, he's not done with you yet, there will be joy." Now that is assurance for my mind and heart.

One of my all-time favorites is "Goodness of God." by Jenn Johnson of Bethel Worship. Lines like "all my life you have been faithful, you have walked me through the fire, and I will sing of the goodness of God." Wow, just Wow!

I was blessed with an opportunity to be on a worship team. Without sounding biased, this team was incredibly gifted. Our worship leader has a voice that to this day causes me to cry, smile, and every other emotion. When she sang Goodness of God, I felt like an inner explosion occurred in the best way. I lose myself in those moments. That is the beauty of music.

I could go on and on about music and what moves me, but what about you? What song or songs stop you in your tracks? God gave us voices to use and ands to play instruments. He gives us sweet moments to just stop, listen, feel, and be. Allow yourself to be moved by the music.

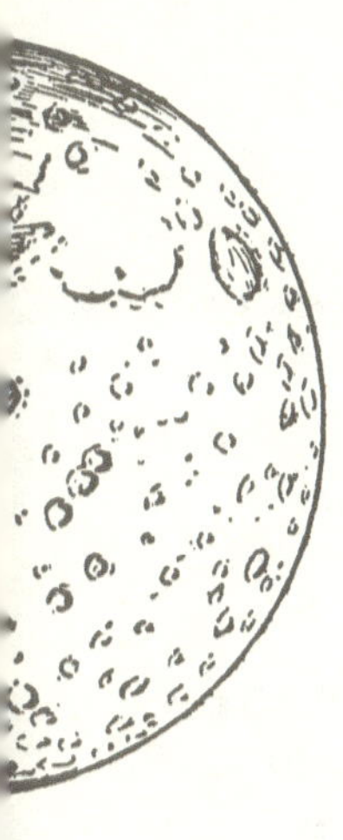

REFLECTION:

Day 7...Morning

CHERISHED TRADITIONS

For where two or three are gathered in My name, there I am in their midst. Matthew 18:20

Traditions vary from family to family. Since my family is either scattered or deceased my traditions may seem different. Like a memory of mom making her holiday stuffed mushrooms and mumbling. She always prepared more than we needed. Or when my dad took us to a fancy restaurant in New York City to celebrate a special occasion. My stepmother still sends an ornament each Christmas season from somewhere she has visited and it is placed on our tree. These are all traditions I treasure in memory.

Some new traditions have emerged, filling my heart greatly. One is a weekly dinner with my daughter while my husband is working. These mom/daughter dates allow us to share time and life. She does more of the talking it seems and I do more listening. But I get a few interjections here and there. I am grateful that she even wants to spend time with me as many young adults want to hang out with their friends, not their parents. Sometimes a friend or two joins us and it seems they all have much to say.

Another tradition that has become a sweet treat to my life is a weekly date with my husband and my daughter, we three will play cards or board games, cook a meal together, watch a sporting event or go on the boat to do some fishing. We all look forward to these little adventures whether we are home or out. Time goes so fast!

So many parents have expressed wanting time with their adult children and often do not get that as often as they like. My hope and prayer are that everyone gets to have a wonderful family tradition whether it is something small and simple, or big and luxurious. My heart is blessed with the traditions I am living. Traditions come and some go. May the ones meant to stay live on, and new ones be welcomed as they surface. Scripture talks about honoring our parents, loving each other and sharing time together. It also tells us to speak of God's word. What tradition fills your heart and brings God into the midst?

REFLECTION:

Day 7...Evening

CHERISHED TRADITIONS

Everyone who loves had been born of God and knows God. 1John 4:8

It may sound silly, but we've always had Huggy Kissy Parties. When our kids were little, my husband began this unique tradition because no matter how many time-outs and tantrums they had, we wanted them to know they were loved. Their over-tired, wiggling little bodies would settle down after a session of this engaging game.

This tradition consisted of everyone gathering in a circle and hugging each other, while delivering countless kisses to our family members simultaneously. Parents, siblings, and everyone were included. One rule that made it more fun was you couldn't be slow. This was family bonding at full speed. We never kept score, but I can assure you that no one ever left feeling unloved.

Huggy Kissy Parties did not happen as often as we cruised into the turbulent teen years of rebellion and heartbreak. Busy schedules and different interests made it harder to come together. When hurt feelings and disagreements popped up, words of affirmation were the key in keeping communication going between all members of our family. It may not have always been pretty, but the result was forgiveness and restoration, which was my goal regardless of how we got there.

I look forward to seeing my daughter, her husband, and my new grandbaby. How wonderful it will be to have a Huggy Kissy Party with them and hear the giggles coming from the youngest member of our esteemed club. My hope is that these parties continue down the family line, and for generations to come.

Huggy Kissy Parties remind me how deeply we are loved by our Creator. We may stumble and act unlovable, but be assured, when we repent, He is always ready to forgive us. His arms are always ready to embrace and shower us with His endless grace. Do you think there are Huggy Kissy Parties in heaven? I sure hope so.

REFLECTION:

"God said, "Let there be light," and there was light. God saw that the light was good, and he separated the light from the darkness. God called the light "day," and the darkness he called "night." And there was evening, and there was morning—the first day."

Genesis 1:3–5

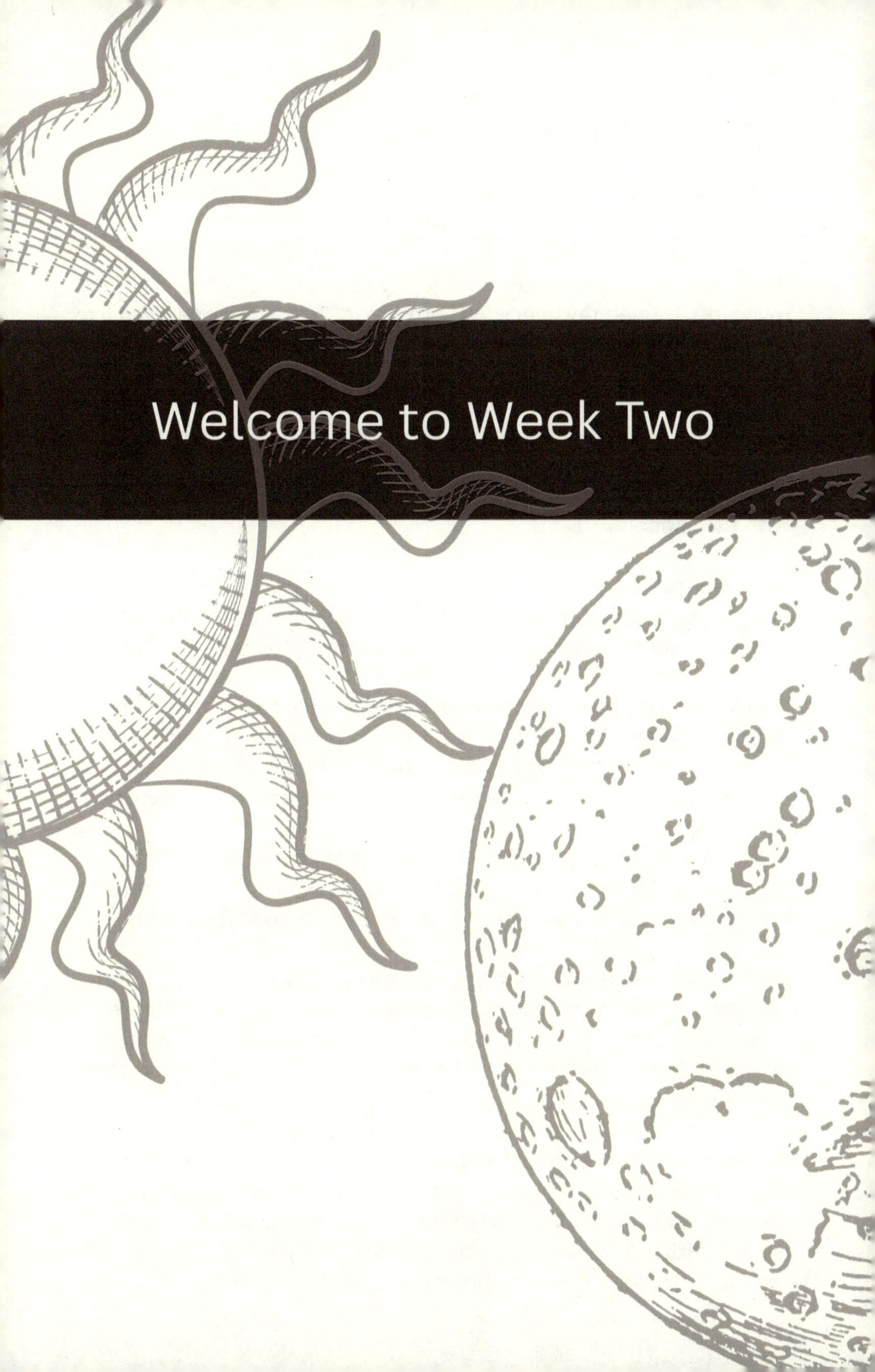

Welcome to Week Two

Day 8...Morning

A WHIRLWIND OF COURAGE

You will keep in perfect peace those whose minds are steadfast, because they trust in you. Isaiah 26:3

Peace was a word that was completely foreign to me. Anxiety ruled my world. It filled my everyday with dread. To be calm, seemed like an unattainable goal. A dream that others only get to live.

What I didn't understand then was that it is possible to have peace, even when dealing with panic or an unexpected crisis. Peace does not come from the environment you find yourself in. It comes from trusting God with the unknown. It comes from being comfortable with the "uncomfortable."

Have I gotten where peace reigns in my heart 24/7? It would be lying if I told you that was the case. However, my roller coaster life has given me plenty of practice in finding peace in the middle of chaos.

God's peace is not hidden; it is always available to us. It may take digging through the layers of lies we have believed, to find it. By turning to Jesus, reading His Word, hearing inspiring music, and using tools for battling anxiety, we can reclaim our peaceful thoughts.

In this calmer phase, it is possible to exchange the "What if's" we fear, to the "So What?" So, what if my life is not what I planned it to be?" There are still joyful moments of peace to look forward to.

We have not been promised stress-free living without any hiccups. The sooner we realize this truth, the easier it is to accept that real peace only comes from one source, God. Yes, we can use strategies and tools but deep down if we don't know Him, we will always feel like something is missing.

It takes courage to admit that we don't have it all together, but it is in that confession where God can begin to rebuild us. God can make us stronger and wiser in how we handle worry and anxiety. The next time negative thoughts try to take over, stand your ground and remind them that God has your back.

REFLECTION:

Day 8... Evening

WHIRLWIND OF COURAGE

Be strong and courageous. Joshua 1:9

My former self is probably very confused with this person I have become. However, admittedly, it still baffles me sometimes, but I truly like who I am. All of it from an unforeseen battle that I walked through or should say crawled through. Yet, out of the fire came a warrior for God.

What a whirlwind the last sixteen years have been. In the past, I was all about my career. Doing life by the demands of the flesh so to say and living according to society's trends. As a wife, mother and business owner I had a full plate. Add in the needs of others and it certainly caught up with me. My world came crashing down in a heap at my feet. I was now facing an illness that could take my very life.

Jumping into action was a natural response for me. In my strength and power, I would get nowhere, yet with God I had a fighting chance. So that is exactly where I turned, in prayer, in frustration and desperation. For the first time in my life, I did not have control and that brought me to my knees.

God met me where I was. He heard my cries and filled me with a supernatural strength I know full well only came because of Him. I rose up with courage determined to not be taken out. God was in that fire with me and walked me through the toughest of days.

I have gone from a worldly perspective of career driven to doing ministry. Surrendering was key and the outcome has been nothing short of amazing. Now as a published author, I write encouraging words and watch people find hope again. All I am, and all that has come to be, is all to the credit of the Lord.

So, whatever you are facing, walking through or running from, know that you are never alone. " Do not be afraid, do not be discouraged, for the Lord, your God will be with you wherever you go." Joshua 1:9 NIV He was with me and I trust He is with you too. God has this!

REFLECTION:

Day 9...Morning

LESSONS LEARNED

Everyone should be quick to listen, slow to speak and slow to become angry. James 1:19

Lessons are lessons for a reason. We go through them in all seasons of our lives. Let's face it, lessons are defining moments, stirred up in the never-ending cycle of the world. Yet it is in those long and grueling times that we can process the truth of each lesson and what we learned from them.

In my quiet moments, I thought about the barrage of things I experienced this past week. There were beautiful, tender and exciting times, however, there were some tough ones for my heart to handle and well, I broke.

The dam let loose and anger and hurt surfaced. But God! The One and only in all his glory was by my side. I spoke out a lot, it was not pretty by any means yet, necessary. The rawness felt deep within, but I could feel his presence which comforted me greatly. The time spent still took me to place of gratitude. Yes, it showed me how so many are hurting and that becomes a pattern to put onto someone else. That someone else was me, sad, but true. You have heard the saying, “Hurting people hurt people.”

I am a giver, a helper, and a motivator, however sometimes that kicks me in the rear. This latest experience left me feeling betrayed and I wanted to roar, I wanted justice. So human! But, instead of calling it out for what I felt it was, silence took over.

My mind raced and rumbled, “What now God?” Then I waited and waited. Turns out what I thought was done in an underhanded way was not the case. Keeping my mouth shut was the best option to avoid unnecessary conflict. Staying quiet when I thought I had grounds to shout from the rooftops is a true lesson learned.

What lessons have you learned recently? In Scripture, we are told to be quick to listen, slow to speak and slow to anger. Can you imagine how many conflicts would not occur if we followed this instruction?

REFLECTION:

Day 9...Evening

LESSONS LEARNED

I praise you because I am fearfully and wonderfully made... Psalm139:14

Life experiences can distort who we are leaving us searching for acceptance. I tried different ways to find my worth, but it didn't work. When the scars of the past are tattooed on your heart, it is easy to fall into the trap of feeling worthless. You stop trying; instead, you end up swallowing every lie the enemy shoots your way.

My life changing revelation happened as I took the time to study the Bible. It is filled with people who didn't think much of themselves. Many were sick, pushed aside, and invisible to others. Jesus had unwavering compassion and love for them. John 3:16 states that God covered in flesh was willing to die for of us. That included me, so my worth is sealed in Him. Suddenly, there was no need to have the approval of others, or even myself. From then on, Jesus became my focal point. He is where all my self-esteem derives from.

The image in the mirror changed. There was untapped beauty hidden behind my skewed reflection. This child of the King had been imprisoned far too long because of lies and criticism. Though the enemy wanted to silence me, I was ready to experience real freedom. Through God's redeeming grace, I found the courage to speak in front of a crowd, publish my words, and share myself with others. It was no longer about me, but about reflecting Jesus. When we put Him first and follow His agenda, His royal blood washes over all our insecurities.

I can say with conviction, "You've come a long way baby." It is true the hands of time have added a few more wrinkles and a few pounds here and there. However, my interior had a full makeover. My self-esteem got an upgrade, and it came with perks! It's never too early or too late to get a Jesus makeover!

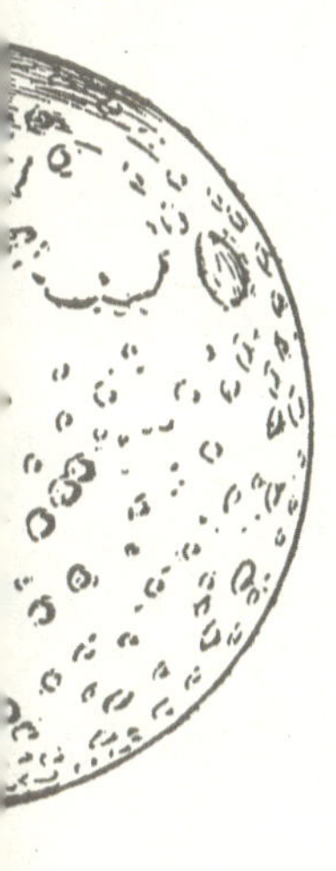

REFLECTION:

Day 10... Morning

BOUNCE BACK

"...for the Lord your God goes with you, He will never leave you nor forsake you." Deuteronomy 31:6

Sometimes, we want something so intensely that we blind ourselves to the truth. That was me. A naive teen, head over heels with what I thought was the prince of my dreams, attractive and sweet. My adolescent knees turned to jelly when he said my name. I never imagined the trouble that relationship could bring.

It was not long before puppy love turned into manipulation. "Don't wear that skirt, your legs are too skinny." Many of his remarks wounded me, but I was mesmerized by his pearly whites and ocean blue eyes. Regardless of what my friends said, the last thing I wanted to accept was that I had fallen for the wrong guy.

Mind games followed. His threats to kill himself if I left him, the alligator tears, and the promises that only lasted for a short while, kept me trapped. I was young and gullible, his lies weighed heavy on my heart. I was blinded to the truth. He was a Narcissist who enjoyed making me suffer.

His words after our breakup were, "No one will ever love you like I do." Those words seeped into my mind like poison. My world fell apart as my heart shattered. I stopped eating and barely slept. I prayed he would call me to tell me he couldn't live without me and mean it this time. But thank the Lord, my prayers only hit the ceiling.

Time passed, another young man came into my life. He mended my heart and taught me how to trust and what real love should look like. Six and a half years later, he became my husband.

I know it was God's protection that covered me that day, because Narcissists rarely give up. They may play with their prey, but they seldom set them free. If you are in a similar situation, please seek help. God is with you and He has a better plan for your life. One of real, authentic love with no strings attached.

REFLECTION:

Day 10...Evening

BOUNCE BACK

"When I am afraid, I put my trust in you." Psalm 56:3

July 2010, life crashed around me. A phone call with words I did not want to hear but had to face. You have cancer. BAM-slap down! Where do I go with that? Well, right into prayer is where. At first, I cried and then cried some more. Words rolled around in my head and my mouth mumbled but made no sense. Until I realized I was so lost in this devastating news that I could not even speak. Time was what I needed, even though time was not on my side.

And so it began, the daily grind, turned into a battle to survive. Prayer and support from family and friends gave me the strength and courage.. I had hard decisions to make regarding my health and my business. Well, that's a no-brainer, health comes first!

Basically, I let go and let God. Just like that, for it had to be done. I mourned giving up my business. What I gained was so much better, a second chance in life. With it came much uncertainty, yet it brought a level of faith, of closeness, I had not experienced before.

Life was a roller coaster with ups and downs, good and bad days along with a mountain of debt. However, I learned to lay it down, give it to God and trust his plan. I packed up the old me. These days I teach a workshop to help others lay it down and pack their suitcases up with old habits, hurts and hindrances. For better days to come and miracles do happen. I am living proof.

I have no doubt whatsoever that God walked each mile with me. I prayed it, spoke it, cried many tears, and laid awake into the nights waiting for Him to speak. I thought I was running out of time and yet, God showed me the beauty of time He gives through His mercy and grace.

Are you facing uncertainty and wonder if you have time? Talk with the Lord, tell Him everything and then wait. He hears and He makes time.

REFLECTION:

Day 11...Morning

FUTURE HOPE

"As iron sharpens iron, so one person sharpens another." Proverbs 27:17

It feels like a lifetime ago, but about two decades have passed since I was a private investigator. Not to boast, but I was good at it. Many years of watching crime shows taught me how to figure out who did it rather quickly.

I have been what is called a Jackie of all trades. While facing a roadblock in life, I considered the police academy. Then I saw an ad for a PI course. So, I applied and got accepted. Having worked in mental health as a case manager, and as an intern for children's services, I was no stranger to this world of dysfunctional living. My BA degree, plus work history moved the process along and I was grandfathered in.

A door had opened. An instructor in the course noticed my assertiveness and presented me with a job opportunity. He witnessed me locate the weapon used in a crime drill and complimented me in front of my peers. I was elated while my peers smirked, but that is life.

I went through the process of becoming a licensed investigator within the state of Florida. A new adventure had begun. I had so much to learn. Yet, being guided by a well-respected investigator and agency owner was a plus. He saw something in me even when I did not. Before long, I proved him right.

I am extremely appreciative of the investment made in me. Years have passed, my former boss and I parted ways, I opened my own agency as he advanced his. All in all, it was a good thing, a turning point I am grateful for!

God puts mentors in our lives for encouragement and guidance. Do you have a mentor? Or perhaps, you are a mentor. God knows the plan and we His people are here with a purpose.

REFLECTION:

Day 11...Evening

FUTURE HOPE

There is surely a future hope for you, and your hope will not be cut off. Proverbs 23:18

High school teachers have the power to push you toward your future or stop you. Words can be used to build up a student or knock them from the teenage tight rope they walk on.

I had an honors English teacher in my senior year who looked at my diamond in the rough stories and saw a future author. He gave me extra writing assignments. When I made mistakes, he would correct me, but in the same breath, he would praise me. Criticism was part of my daily life back then. I wasn't smart enough, I wasn't pretty enough. That teacher saw past my self-esteem issues, and gave me hope.

He pushed me to enter writing contests and explore different genres. If I had him as a teacher for a longer time, I think he would have inspired me to go directly into a writing career.

After High School, my secretarial jobs required writing and my Paralegal career taught me research skills. Both were vitally important to becoming a self-published author.

Though I can't remember my teacher's name, I can picture him. He was short, pencil thin, and wore polyester shirts with bell bottom pants. His eyes fixed on my words, a blue pen twirling in hand, as he decorated my assignments with helpful suggestions.

I wonder what he would say today if he knew I became an author? He would say something to the effect of, "Miss Leon, I knew you always had it in you."

God puts people in our paths to steer us in the right direction. We may take detours, but if it is part of God's perfect plan, the road will lead us to where we are destined to be. Where is God leading you to? Who is He using to get you there?

REFLECTION:

Day 12...Morning

GUT FEELING

If we confess our sins, he is faithful and just and will forgive us our sins..." 1 John 1:9

Tired from trying to find the right dress for an event, I sat down in the food court to eat my lunch. Across from me sat this older woman
alone, her meal untouched. I felt that familiar tug. The Holy Spirit was trying to coax me out of my comfort zone.

There were hundreds of reasons why I couldn't ask this stranger to eat with me. The main one was, insecurity wrapped in shyness. Ignoring it didn't work. It only got stronger and would not subside. It came down to obedience and trust. I had to act.

When I asked her, she didn't hesitate. To my utter amazement, the conversation flowed effortlessly. Then somewhere between hello and the weather, she blurted out the secret she had been carrying for years. During her first pregnancy, she had an abortion. That is when I knew this was much more than a gut feeling. This was a divine appointment.

What this sweet soul didn't know was that I volunteered for a crisis pregnancy center to help women choose life. In her guilt and shame, she had alienated her family. Her rationale was that she was evil. She didn't deserve to be a mother to the daughter she currently had. Digging deeper I discovered that she believed God hated her and she would never be forgiven. I assured her Jesus loved her and had died for all her sins, all she had to do was ask to be forgiven. In her tear-filled eyes, I saw hope and relief. Chains were broken that day, and a seed was planted.

I never saw her again, but that stirring in my soul served to bless this woman. God loves all of us all regardless of our sins, God never turns away a heart that has truly repented. If you get that kind of relentless nudging, don't analyze it; don't ignore it. Answer God's calling today and watch him work through you!

REFLECTION:

Day 12...Evening

GUT FEELING

"Thus, by their fruit you will recognize them." Matthew 7:20

I was sitting in a group, desiring to learn more about God's word. Someone asked a question, the leader of the group went to answer, however, another person attending took the reins. From the first word I got a sick feeling in my stomach. As she kept speaking, I closed my eyes and heard some kind of murmuring. It did not sound right.

My mind was alarmed, eyes shut, I saw a vision of a wolf snarling. I could feel its hot breath and smell its saliva. It leaped forward knocking me backwards in my chair. I ran for the bathroom. I was violently ill, sweating and shaking. Not a pretty sight I assure you.

A friend came to check on me. When I came out, I saw the look on her face, then I saw my own reflection in the mirror. horrified and pale. She helped steady me and confirmed what I had experienced was not good. And not of God.

She took me to the altar in the sanctuary. I heard her words and tongues. I had no fear and was thankful she was by my side. Another friend approached and knelt with us. He also prayed and spoke in tongues. I was surrounded with love and protection. The three of us sat quietly, then he explained what had occurred. Sharing that every time the door opens for people to walk in, the enemy finds a way in too. This experience is one I don't want to repeat. I chose to leave the group, as did a few others. Yet I am grateful for those friends.

On a good note, I now speak in tongues since praying and asking God to gift me with no fear. I have become in tune with what is of God and what is not. Scripture is ripe with words of discernment and tells us to put on the full armor of God daily. Have you had a gut feeling of caution? Turn to God in prayer and ask for His protection. He can and will keep you from harm.

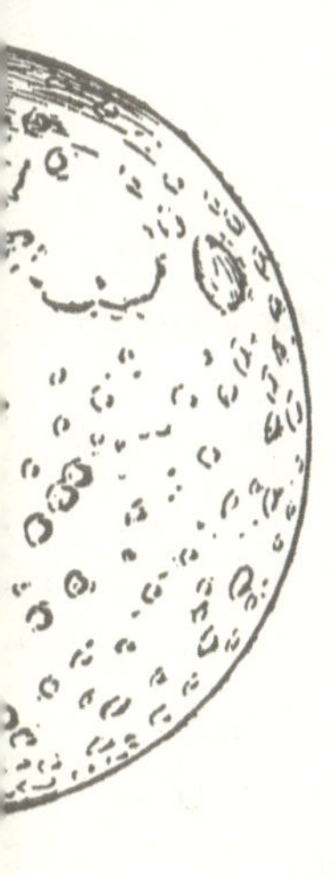

REFLECTION:

Day 13...Morning

TOUCHING THE HEART THROUGH FILM

"Then you will know the truth, and the truth will set you free." John 8:32

So many movies, so much popcorn, where do I begin?

My pen still, paper ready, as my mind flashed images of movies I have watched over the past decades of my life. The question I ask myself is what single movie truly inspired me. I gather if I dig deep enough, I could create a long list, but one came to the surface.

"Erin Brockovich" on screen in 2000, starring Julia Roberts, was a real life or as real life as Hollywood could get legal drama. This film showed a woman who took on a major corporation linked to water contamination. She stood courageous despite all the attempts to discredit her. Acts of harassment and threats of harm did not deter her. Instead, she pressed forward to prove the company's actions had caused terminal illness to people in the community.

Julia Roberts did a great job and if memory serves me right, she won an award for her character role. However, Erin, the woman portrayed in the film, incredibly inspired me as she walked it, talked it, lived it and let's not forget exposed it. If more of us were willing to do this, wow, much of what happens daily would not stand a chance. Erin is my kind of lady!

The Word is full of scripture that says speak truth and speak life. Every word out of our mouths either lifts or destroys someone. I feel I am one that steps up and speaks up, my former career and my books prove that to be true. Perhaps this movie back in 2000 helped mold me into a woman of truth. For what we see and hear does impact our minds and lives.

What truth have you witnessed? What truth have you spoken? May today be a day that inspires you to walk it, talk it, and live it so someone, somewhere can look back and say, "that inspired me."

REFLECTION:

Day 13...Evening

TOUCHING THE HEART THROUGH FILM

He is the atoning sacrifice for our sins, and not only for ours but also for the sins of the whole world. 1 John 2:2

There are movies that challenge our thoughts, and teaches lessons that stay with us long after the movie ends. For me, The Shack was one of those movies. Apart from some controversial aspects, this movie had a scene that explained hard truths. Mack, the main character, is consumed by hatred he has for the murderer who killed his young daughter. In a poignant scene, Wisdom, shows Mack the horrible abuse that man faced as a young child and what drove him to become an unfeeling monster.

Mack's thirsts for revenge charges God with being unjust and unloving. Since Mack thinks he knows how to judge others, Wisdom gives him the chance to play God and judge evil. Then she makes him choose between his two children. Who will he send to Hell and who will stay? Mack is outraged, but he must choose. Wisdom helps him weigh the options by pointing out the misbehavior of both children. Which one is more disobedient? Which deserves to be punished? Like any loving parent, he can't choose. He tells Wisdom to send him to Hell instead.

Now, Mack grasps God's perfect love for all mankind. God in the flesh sacrificially went to the cross so we could be absolved of our sins. Jesus died for those who do good, evil, and everyone in between. We won't comprehend the fullness of God's love on this side of eternity. That is why we are told to trust Him.

The movie takes a horrible thing like the murder of an innocent child, and through an encounter with God, Mack finds his healing. This creates a domino effect that helps his grieving family cope as well.

Movies touch us in different ways. We need to be careful what we watch. So scary, dark, or violent, movies are out of the question for me. Instead give me some inspiring film that feeds my soul, a bucket of popcorn, and you got my attention. What movies touch your heart?

REFLECTION:

Day 14...Morning

AROUND THE CLOCK SUPPORT

A friend loves at all times, and a brother is born for adversity. Proverbs 17:17

I call her my "angel." She is someone who blessed our family. When my son was having multiple non-stop, Tourette's Syndrome episodes, we tried every neurologist in the East Coast. Even the prestigious experts couldn't help. Desperate, I posted on a Tourette Facebook page my son's dilemma. Seconds later, this helpful woman, contacted me. Her son was being seen by a specialist on the West Coast. She offered to call and ask if they would see our son.

This specific center uses the most up to date, scientific proven neurological treatments. Normally, it takes six months or longer to get an appointment. Thank the Lord who moves mountains, her call back consisted of one question, "Could we be there at 8 a.m. the following morning?"

The Ronald McDonald house in St Petersburg, Florida, became our home for four draining weeks. Our son got the beneficial therapies needed without the added stress of traveling. During the first session we were warned this therapy would be challenging for our whole family. The selfless angel who had helped us get into the clinic offered to take my daughter to live with them temporarily. It could not have been more perfect! Our daughters were the same age, and it was during summer break. Pool time, ice cream runs, and movies, kept my girl entertained.

In this life, I could never repay her kindness or the friendship we share. Though our kids are all grown and she has moved away to another state, we keep in touch. Someday I hope to visit her and escape to our favorite restaurant.

I know beyond a shadow of a doubt, that God sent this angel wrapped in skin and her family to lead us to the right place, at the right time. God still does miracles, and earthly angels walk among us. If you look, you will find angels in your life too.

REFLECTION:

Day 14...Evening

AROUND THE CLOCK SUPPORT

"Never will I leave you; never will I forsake you." Hebrews 13:5

More times than not I am that friend that helps when needed. That is what friends do. However, my friend/neighbor came to my rescue one night when I was not feeling well. I was home by myself and had pain in my chest and down my left arm. Not knowing what to do and not wanting to be alone as my husband works nights, I called her. She came over within seconds, took my blood pressure and asked me some questions. After seeing how high my numbers were, she dialed 911. Then helped me change into more appropriate pajamas and put my dogs out so the paramedics could enter safely.

As the red flashing lights arrived, she opened the door and let out a gasp. Six paramedics/firefighters walked up to my house. "Kim, oh my gosh, it's a real-life fireman calendar!" Even though I was short of breath I just had to laugh. One by one they entered, did my vitals and had me chew baby aspirins. I was put on a stretcher and placed inside an ambulance. This was my first ride and hopefully my last ride in a emergency vehicle. My neighbor was concerned for me but was also amused by how many had shown up. She called my family and got the dogs settled.

I was admitted into the hospital even though my symptoms and test results were not life threatening. However, observation was highly recommended. In came my neighbor to sit with me until my husband was in route. That is friendship to the tee!

When I was resting at home, she came over. We busted out laughing as we recalled that night. Her son is a firefighter who could easily be on a calendar. Then the thought hit me, had we not changed my pajamas those six men would have gotten quite a sight! But in their line of work, I am sure they have seen it all.

Has there been a time of need and someone came to your rescue? God is always with us. Rest assured, He never forsakes us.

REFLECTION:

Let the morning bring me word
of your unfailing
love, for I have put my trust in
you. Show me
the way I should go for to you I
entrust my life.
Psalm 143:8

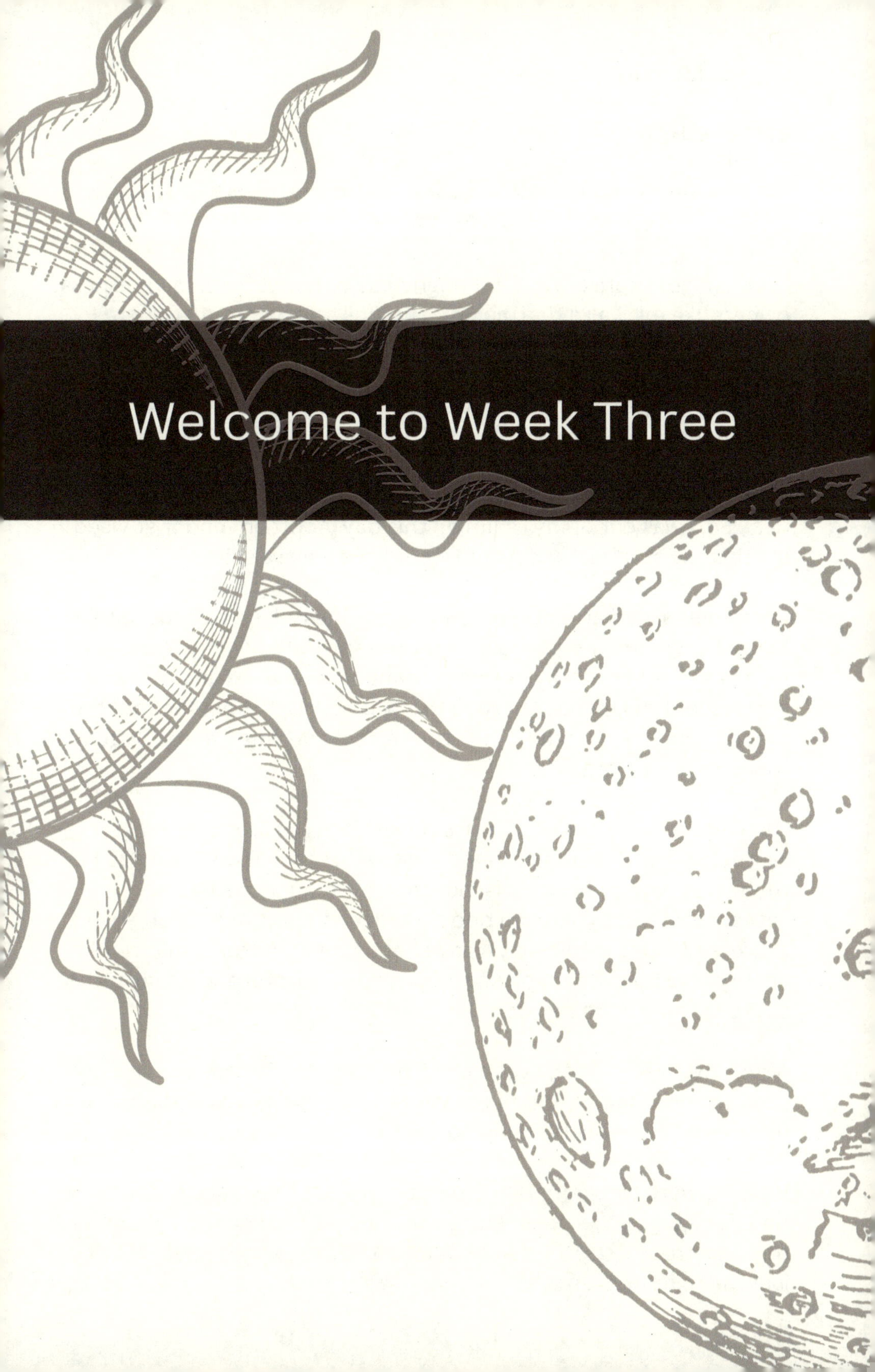

Welcome to Week Three

Day 15...Morning

BLESSED BY A STRANGER

"A generous person will prosper; whoever refreshes others will be refreshed." Proverbs 11:25

I got a huge surprise. What I thought was an event for small business owners like me was a flea market, aka junk sale, yet that is where I met a stranger.

My table was covered with books, journals and other merchandise, all were new. The tables all around me, well, their items were not. Many looked at my table, smiled and kept going. Some customers complimented me; however, they were seeking that great bargain deal. So, I was out of my realm on this day. Another vendor advised me that my stuff was nice, but I would not make a sale.

Until I met a woman with gorgeous eyes. She walked right up with a big smile. We exchanged hellos and she started opening my books, feeling the covers of my journals, trying on bracelets and smelling my leather bookmarks. My gosh this was my kind of person for I do exactly what she just did. I love to see, feel and smell things. A good friend says I am organic.

Her voice was confident, "This is refreshing, you are refreshing!" I was delighted. She was perhaps the exact reason I was meant to be there. Not only by her words, but then by her actions. As she gathered up a copy of each book, a bracelet and a journal she expressed being in ministry. I gave her some items for a children's charity. You reap what you sow is shared in scripture, advising us not to grow weary in doing good.

About two weeks later, I got a call from this new friend. She saw my post on social media and purchased two specialty boxes for a charity fundraiser. A double blessing no doubt.

Here we were two complete strangers in the same place at the same time for a bigger purpose than either of us knew. For such a time as this. Has there been a time in your life that a stranger appeared at just the right moment?

REFLECTION:

Day 15...Evening

BLESSED BY A STRANGER

"Let each of you look not only to his own interests, but also to the interest of others." Philippians 2:4

After falling flat on my face while walking to my car from a fast-food restaurant, I had little hope for mankind. Glasses, purse, and my dignity, were sprawled all over the pavement. Everyone in the drive through drove past me like I was invisible; all were oblivious to my pain. One young man stopped his car briefly and asked me if I needed help. When I answered, he sped out of the parking lot leaving me in a cloud of engine exhaust.

Someone must have alerted the establishment. An employee came to see why I was lying on the ground. She offered no assistance, but stood there unmoved, watching me struggle to get up. Once I managed to stand up, she quickly handed me a bag of ice for my bloody knees and ran back to her post by the pick-up window. As I hobbled to my car, anger rose inside me. How could people be so cruel?

My irritation was quickly snuffed out by something that happened two days later. My daughter had gone to her voice lessons and lost her wallet. We searched everywhere we could think to look. Hours later, there was a knock at my door. A striking woman with a sweet smile asked if my daughter was home. The helpful stranger had found her lost wallet in the shopping center parking lot. To my daughter's relief, not one dollar was missing, and neither was her ATM card. Even her change had not been touched. This woman could have taken the wallet, instead drove it to our home. Unlike the people at the restuarant, she did the right thing.

We live in a fast-paced world where being a Good Samaritan is overlooked and ridiculed. Her kindness served as a true example of honesty and watching out for the other humans we share this space with. That turned this angry heart not only into a thankful heart, but one who knows God always uses people willing to be His hands and feet.

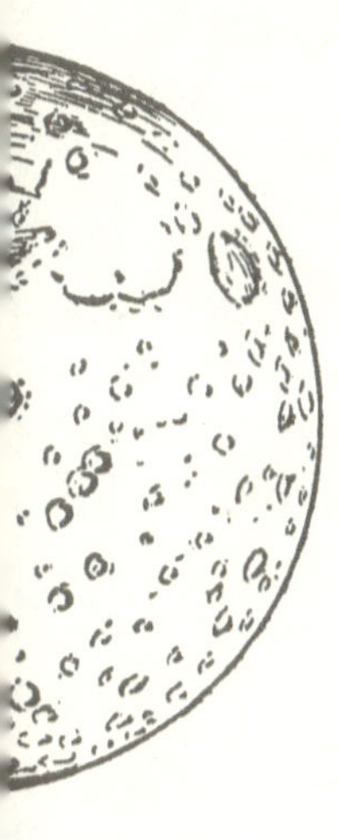

REFLECTION:

Day 16...Morning

TREASURED KEEPSAKE

For nothing will be impossible with God. Luke 1:37

Time has faded the corners, but the smiles still touch my heart. Regardless of their age and condition, they are priceless! Discolored paper squares hold my ancestors, my heritage, and important memories. They bridge the gap from a time I lived in Cuba, but was too young to remember. These voiceless photographs provide scattered puzzle pieces of my upbringing. When I place them side by side, a story of my early years unfolds.

Frozen in time, was the laughter of the youngest members of my family, yet unaware of the financial and emotional strain our parents faced. A blurry shot of my beloved plastic doll, beneath my baby carriage. The same plastic doll, that years later, I left to another little girl. I can still remember the promise that my father made me, "Where we are going, you will have many dolls."

Yellowed black and white photos of fruit trees, and historic buildings, the perfect back drop to display their vacations before the iron grip of Communism took over the land. Snapshots of celebrations, graduations, weddings, birthdays, and festive reunions. So many memories locked away in the pensive looks, and hopeful smiles. We are united by blood and similar features yet never shared a single word. All of us, captured by the muted flash of the light bulb of an old-fashioned camera.

Modern technology continues to document my life's journey in digital form. Each vivid color visual is stamped by the grace and mercy of a loving God. When I was too young to understand, He made a way for me to leave behind what would be darkness and oppression.

I don't have a picture-perfect life, who does? But no matter where you come from or where you are in life, you can trust Him with your past, your present, and your future. God always has a purpose that far exceeds anything you can see in a photograph.

REFLECTION:

Day 16...Evening

TREASURED KEEPSAKE

He refreshes my soul. Psalm 23:3

I am not big on material things, never have been. However, I was given a pair of diamond studs that my paternal grandmother wanted me to have. I wear them almost daily. She is deceased, we were not close, still, I am grateful.

An item I have which holds a sentimental place in my heart is my mother's jewelry box. She did not have expensive items like my grandmother, but her old-fashioned wooden box makes me smile. When mom was alive that box held an assortment of costume pieces. Also, a few real pieces she would wear on special occasions. Despite not having financial wealth, she always looked well put together.

After she passed, I sat in her room and looked at her stuff. Something inspired me to gift others, so I bagged up outfits, jewelry, handbags and shoes. A friend displayed all of it at a church luncheon. The ladies gathered up what they could use. Many remarked it made them feel close to my mom.

I chose to keep a few items and her jewelry box. There are three grandchildren, each have been gifted a token of her. The box was emptied and reminded me that mom was no longer physically here. Yet, she was the jewel in life, not the items. Her box holds my collection now and will one day go on to my daughter. I have started to give away my material items. Whatever remains when I am no longer here, I hope my daughter will continue blessing others.

People are the jewels in life and items are mere accessories! A keepsake reminds us of those passed and our hearts hold the memories. Do you have a keepsake that you treasure?

God gave His Son as a precious gift that gave us life. Let that be the keepsake that remains in our hearts and on our minds. Jesus is the ultimate treasured keepsake for all times.

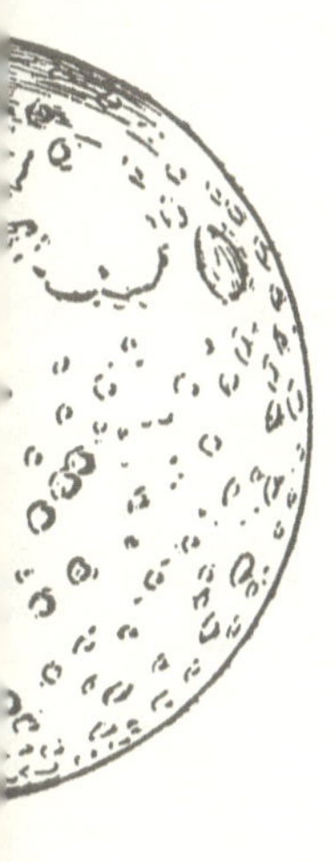

REFLECTION:

Day 17...Morning

FROM OLD TO NEW

Therefore, if anyone is in Christ, the new creation has come. 2 Corinthians 5:17

A small habit or rather a big habit I had to work at is slowing down to spend time on self-care. Sitting and being still led to hearing and seeing. It also led to me not needing or wanting to be in charge at the helm or having the desire to be everywhere for everyone.

This did not happen overnight. Nor did it come easy, but I sit here right now, relaxed, thankful for all that surrounds me. I am quite content. This new habit of self-care has truly balanced me. What a great change in so many ways. My mind is more focused than ever before. Don't get me wrong, I have always been sharp and quick with ideas, however the pressure and stress that usually accompany the task is long gone. No regrets and no looking back.

This all sounds so perfect, doesn't it? Yet, the path was grueling, downright ugly to be honest. Anyone who has been through transformation would agree the hardest part is admitting change is necessary. Stepping up with courage to face what needs to be worked on is where it can get messy. Yes, the support of our family and friends is a benefit in the process, if you can receive it without feeling attacked.

I have found the best tool to use is scripture. Everything we feel and do is expressed on every page of the Bible. Reading words that encourage and motivate positive change is so inspiring. It is the written coach that provides strength to overcome the obstacles and habits I have allowed to stick around for too long.

Are you tired of the habits that detour your path in life? I suggest you open the good book, give it a read and let it do what it was designed to do. Out of the ashes comes beauty, it awaits you. Step up and tap in. The benefits will amaze you as a better way you will find.

REFLECTION:

Day 17...Evening

FROM OLD TO NEW

But as for you, be strong and do not give up, for your work will be rewarded. 2 Chronicles 15:7

You could say I was a "smart phone" late bloomer. While most people used phones for everything, I only used it to text or make calls. Necessity birthed a new habit. Pen and pencil may be old school, but it was effective. The feel of the ink gliding through the paper fueled my creativity. Unfortunately, a swollen arm, cramped hand, and the pain of an old injury made it impossible to keep writing by hand. Typing on the computer was also taxing.

I downloaded a note taking app. Frustration kicked me as the app refused to follow my command. The learning curve took me through tapping on the wrong pull-down menus and even deleting important work. Lots of practice perfected the skill. As a graduate from the newbie status, I experimented with writing whole paragraphs on the app. Scenes started to come together. This dinosaur discovered a painless way to work on long manuscripts.

The same thing happened when I first started reading the Bible. It felt like a chore. Old Testament chapters were about laws and outdated things that didn't make sense the first time I read them. Names were difficult to pronounce. The New Testament brought up more questions than answers. Like, why would they need various books to tell me about Jesus's birth?

I prayed for God to open my understanding. My interest peaked when I discovered that these historical accounts had lessons that could help me in our modern world. Now, my heart was centered on gaining spiritual maturity. My skip and flip method evolved into chapter reading. Words continue to jump off the page year after year.

God's Word is alive. Verses read multiple times add new dimension when you read them with an open mind. Good habits require a time of adaptation. The question is, are you willing to go through the learning process to reap its rewards?

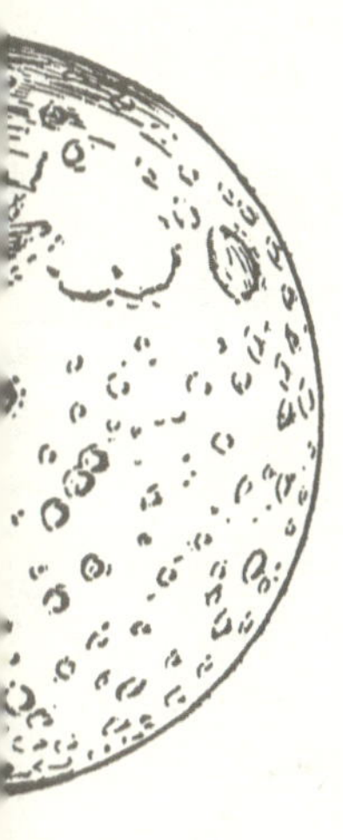

REFLECTION:

Day 18...Morning

IMPACTFUL EXPRESSIONS

Gracious words are like a honeycomb, sweetness to the soul and health to the body. Proverbs 16:24

It seems like today's national sport is to be unkind and fault finding, however, all humans need to be appreciated. As an author making a difference in someone's life, because of something I said or something I wrote, makes my heart dance. It takes courage to put my words out there to be scrutinized, but I will keep on doing it because I know God uses them.

Reviews are great, but when someone personally takes the time to share how they are moved by my books, that energizes my soul. When someone said to my face that they could not get to sleep until they finished my novel, On the Edge of Truth, I was thrilled. The emotions I felt were not because of what they said, but who said it. This individual is not the type who flatters you just to make you feel good. When they speak their mind, they feel it. Therefore, blaming the twist and turns in my plot line for their insomnia was quite a compliment.

Those who have found common ground because I was willing to share my struggles are precious to me. To hear that a reader has clung like a safety net to my self-care book, reminds me that what God inspires me to write, can change lives. It is those brave souls who share how they have found comfort and healing through my Fear Less Living workbook, make my calling to write that much sweeter.

Unsolicited compliments confirm that I have something good to contribute to society. That I have a voice that others need. Through creativity and vulnerability, I can share God's love with those who don't feel seen or heard.

I will keep writing in the hope that many others will react the same way and continue to want to keep reading my page turners. Now is your turn, who can you encourage today?

REFLECTION:

Day 18...Evening

IMPACTFUL EXPRESSIONS

Jesus teaches that "out of the overflow of the heart, the mouth speaks." Matthew 12:34

As a writer I share words daily. Somehow, some way, it will show up. However, during a tough personal season of life I went dormant. With a lot going on in my mind the words were flowing, but not anything I wanted to share. So, I didn't.

While meeting a friend for breakfast, she mentioned missing my words of encouragement as she looked forward to the postings. It gave her a good perspective to take throughout her days. Kindly, I assured her that at some point I would resume but needed this current hiatus. After a wonderful time of catching up we headed out the door, agreeing not to wait so long to meet again.

As we were about to part ways my eyes caught a familiar face and I called out her name. She turned and lit up with her trademark smile. We embraced and out of her mouth came, "I hope everything is okay. I noticed you are not posting any encouraging words these days. Call it selfish, but I need your words to help carry me through my days. Please start again." I looked at my breakfast date, she gave me a wink and a thumbs up. "Funny thing, I just heard this over breakfast." On a crowded walkway we three hugged.

My mind was on go as I walked to my car. Once inside, the engine hummed, the air conditioner blasted my face. I lifted my phone and hit record...Today, it is now, don't waste it.

The gospel shares that we do not know the number of days we have here on earth. Therefore, let's use the time we do have wisely and to spread goodness. Jesus spoke truth in love. Words are powerful and when expressed in kindness, can have great impact on the lives of others as well as our own. Do you look forward to words of encouragement to help you through the days? Or perhaps, you are the one who encourages others. One mouth to one ear and so on, speak life.

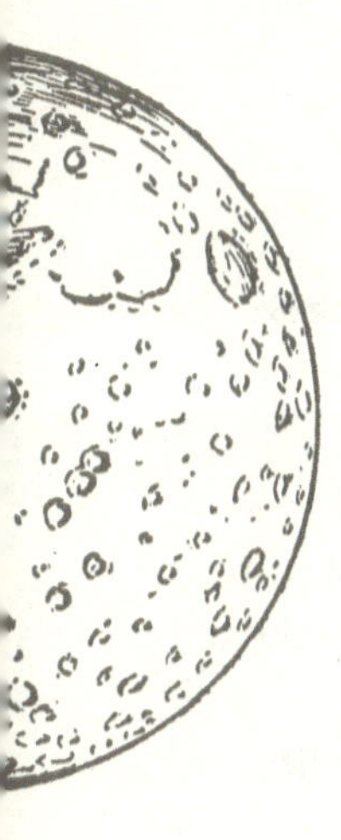

REFLECTION:

Day 19...Morning

1,2,3...

In the beginning, God created the heavens and the earth. Genesis 1:1

I love small and simple things, a variety that could be considered favorites. Right off the top of my head is one thing, the smell of fresh cut grass. To inhale the scent is so pleasing, clean and that makes me smile. Imagine if that smell could be bottled up and sprayed whenever wanted. There is no spray or candle that could replicate that although it has been tried.

Second thing yet it is truly magnificent is the reflection of the sun on water. The ocean, a river, lake or even a pool. Seeing the way the sunlight hits and the ripples flow awes me completely. Add in the sound of the water flowing and it's truly breathtaking.

Third, but not least, for there are so many more I assure you, however I will say laughter. Whether it's deep belly sounds or little giggles it just fills me with joy. I am sure you have noticed this for yourself, if someone starts to laugh, usually it creates a chain reaction. Before long there is much laughter. There is no better sound to the ear and a great rumble in the tummy.

1, 2, 3, these are a few of the things I love about life!

God has given us many things, big and small. His mighty hands created every aspect we know in this world because of His love for His people. With great appreciation for the blessings, we get to experience, let's remember to give Him praise. Scripture tells us countless stories about those who acknowledged that God was the maker, the provider, the healer and so much more. Then we also read about those who took credit for their wellbeing, their land, their wealth and possessions, denying God's hands in all of it.

When thinking of everything our God has given, I throw up my hands in reverence. Each day is a blessing. So go ahead, smell the scents, feel the sun, and laugh until your tummy rumbles. How about you, what three things do you love?

REFLECTION:

Day 19...Evening

1, 2, 3...

I will praise the name of God with a song; I will magnify him with thanksgiving. Ephesians 69:30

If I were to categorize things that bring me joy, the first one would be my grandbaby's face. I could be having a horrible day, but one look at his curious eyes and infectious grin, and nothing else matters. All my problems fade into the innocence of the moment, as my heart melts with love. He is like a soothing wave that washes over the rocky edges of the day. It is easy to unwind blowing raspberries and playing peek-a-boo. This kind of effortless and all compassing love is the kind of love God wants us to feel when we are in His presence. No distractions of worry, fear, or stress from the hardness of life.

The second thing that brings me joy on this earth is chocolate! My name is Ileana, I am a recovering Chocoholic. As a recovering Choco addict I must watch my sugar intake. Moderation is key to good health. However, chocolate will always hold a special place in my heart. I have many fond memories of sharing all things chocolate, with my dear friend who now resides with the Lord.

The third thing that has makes me joyful is teaching. I have taught children and adults alike. My background stems from teaching in homeschool settings and private schools. All children want to learn. If they don't, it is because they have not been given the tools, or they have deficits that require more hands-on techniques. Being creative and fun in the approach, often softens an unwilling child. Adults are more eager to learn because for them the stakes are higher. In the process of teaching both children and adults, I have learned lessons like patience, thinking outside the box, and seeing the potential in them that they don't always see.

We can find great joy in many ways while we are on this planet. But nothing will ever compare to the joy we will have once we depart to our eternal home. What brings you joy? I hope whatever it is, reminds you that God is Jehovah Jireh, our great provider!

REFLECTION:

Day 20...Morning

LAUGHTER FOR THE SOUL

A Cheerful Heart is good medicine...Proverbs 17:22

It was the socially awkward years of middle school I was on the school bus heading home. It was raining. No big deal, right? I mean, a little rain never hurt anyone, unless you were Cuban.

I looked out the school bus window; there she was. A pint-size Speedster, running up to my bus with an oversized bath towel covering her head. As I got off the bus, Super Grandma threw the giant towel over my head and wrapped me up like a burrito. I couldn't see where I was going. Fumming I asked her, "Abuela, you couldn't bring the umbrella?"

To our elder population, getting rained on is extremely dangerous. No Cuban child should ever be exposed to a drop of rain, or they will get very sick. If you got sick, they would lather you with Vicks VapoRub and make you sweat like a little pig, to lower the alleged, "rain-producing fever. That must have been the thought behind my grandmother's brilliant idea.

I did get teased about it, but it didn't last long. I thank God that most of the kids were of Cuban descent and had their fair share of experience with overprotection. Seeing an old lady running like a crazed chicken in the rain, carrying a giant towel, was funny to them, but relatable. Though I would never admit it, inside my dramatic little heart, I appreciated her selflessness. Grandma risked catching the dreaded Rainfall Flu to make sure I didn't. That was huge!

Isn't that how God loves and protects His children? His love has no boundaries. Have you ever felt it? Imagine His big heavenly arms around you and the covering of His grace when you need forgiveness. That's the kind of love that can't be beat.

REFLECTION:

Day 20...Evening

LAUGHTER FOR THE SOUL

"A time to cry and a time to laugh." Ecclesiastes 3:4

While visiting my dad in Lake Tahoe we discovered a critter was getting into the house. How did we know? Well, little droppings were a sign, and a call was made to a pest control company. A time was scheduled, but it would take a few days to get someone out to help.

The house was quite big, four stories with many places for a critter to hide. So, we went about enjoying our family time, paying no mind to what might be among us. Until one evening, while in the theater room watching a movie, we heard screeching and scratching. My dad jumped into action, stopping the movie, turning on the lights, and ushering us out. I scooped up my toddler and left with no hesitation. He, along with my husband, affectionately nicknamed "hey kid" by my father stayed behind to find the critter.

From behind the closed door, we could hear a series of words, not ones I will share. It sounded like a war was transpiring in that movie room. My stepmother walked to the door and opened it up to see what was occurring. I was right behind her and caught a glimpse in. It was quite comical and we could not hold back laughing.

Envision this, dad on one side, my hubby on the other and a flying squirrel in the middle! This was epic but we closed the door to leave the men to handle that crisis. When they finally came out, the look on their faces caused more laughter. We, however, were not laughing at them, but at the situation. They too started to laugh. I wish I could tell you the mission was accomplished, but the furry critter escaped their wrath. And as far as the movie is concerned, well we never did get to see the ending, but who needs movies when real life is so full of adventure.

Times like this remind me that God gave us emotions. Sometimes we cry or get mad, but this time we laughed. Scripture tells us that Jesus too had emotions. Have you had a good laugh lately?

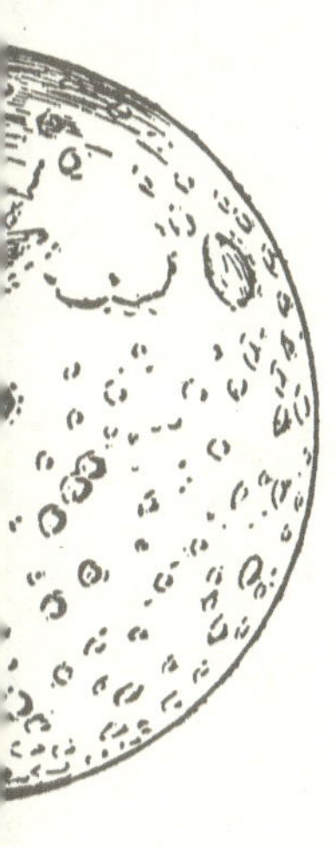

REFLECTION:

Day 21...Morning

UNFORESEEN

For we walk by faith, not by sight. 2 Corinthians 5:7

I had a baby! Yes, I did, rather we did, my husband and me. After trying for so long, with no positive results I felt hopeless. Something I wanted so badly was not happening. I saw doctors, ate right, exercised and got plenty of good sleep, but nothing.

Honestly, I drove my husband nuts with let's try this and that. Even sent him to get tested which he was not thrilled about, but he did it for me. He got thumbs up results so back to square one. What was the problem? I felt the problem was mine.

We prayed, we talked, I cried. He held me. Then one day I just threw my hands up and declared, "Forget this, I am done trying. I am going to concentrate on my career."

I uploaded an online application for the FBI and printed it out. My mind was frustrated and my heart ached. That application sat on my desk and each time I attempted to fill it out something stopped me. I would look at it and not know where to start, so I pushed it aside and walked away.

Battling my thoughts one rainy afternoon, I sat determined to stop feeling sorry for myself and picked up the application and a pen. I started to fill in the spaces, however the pen ink blotched and made a mess of the application. A few words came out at that moment, and I felt angry as well. Then the tears welled up. I attempted to print another application and the printer jammed. I sat there and had a meltdown. A deep and ugly release that helped me to feel better. I rose up from my desk, pitched the pen into the can and crumbled up that application into a ball. Lifting my hand, I gave a free shot and what a shot it was!

I do not know the exact dates between tossing the application and handing my husband a Winnie the Pooh baby rattle, yet I certainly do remember the look on his face. It was priceless. As was the lesson learned – in God's timing, not mine.

REFLECTION:

Day 21...Evening

UNFORSEEN

Being confident of this, that He who began a good work in you will carry it on to completion until the day of Christ Jesus. Philippians 1:6

Faith is believing without any visible evidence to prove it. God is all-powerful, and He has done great things in my life. But when my daughter walked away from the faith, my trust wobbled.

My heart was broken, yet God's still small voice kept telling me that He loved my girl more than I ever could. I had to trust in His perfect timing and stop trying to force the outcome. After days of tearful prayers, I wrote her name on paper, folded it, and put it in my prayer box. Was it easy to give up any claims to my daughter and stop trying to control her life? No! But God had a bigger plan, one than I could have ever imagined. He wanted her soul, her heart, and her devotion, and I was in the way.

The arguments became less when I accepted that it was God's job to change her, not mine. Unfortunately, her calls also became fewer. My hope evaporated with each passing day. Then unexpectedly, she called to tell me that a co-worker had invited her church. I encouraged her to go, but I did not press it further
The following weekend she called again. There was excitement in her voice. Turns out this church was like the church she grew up in. The Pastor even offered her a job teaching Children's church.

The love for the Lord we had planted in her since she was born was blooming again. My daughter recommitted her life to Jesus, was baptized, and started living a more Christ-centered life. Presently, she is married to a pastor, serves in ministry teaching and singing praises to our King Jesus.

Perhaps you are waiting for a prodigal to return, or you might be the prodigal. Luke 15:11-32, reminds us of His relentless love. He never gets tired of waiting. His arms will stay wide open until we are back where we belong.

REFLECTION:

"The day is yours, and
yours also the night;
you established the sun
and moon".
Psalm 74:16

Welcome to Week Four

Day 22...Morning

DREAMS DO COME TRUE

Each of you should use whatever gift you have received to serve others, as faithful stewards of God's grace in its various forms. 1 Peter 4:10

I have had dreams throughout my life that have been fulfilled. Getting married to the man I love and being a mother. There is one dream that I wasn't sure would come true. It was becoming a published author. Writing is my passion but putting my words out there for everyone to read, was a terrifying thought.

Writing my first novel I became personally invested in the lives and emotions of my characters. It was my own creativity that crafted their personalities, gave them names, and gave them scenarios where they could tell a story. They kept me company for a long time, rehearsing dialogue in my mind, and working out the plot holes. They were my creations, my babies. And I am still very protective over them.

There is great excitement in watching the words you write become a physical book that someone can pick up and read. There is something almost miraculous when a manuscript becomes a real book. That first shipment of books that you get to open comes with very happy tears. But its not without ugly tears too.

Writing a manuscript requires multiple re-writes, edits, changes, and deletes. It requires cutting scenes and characters that have become a part of you. Deadlines cause sacrifices that affect family life. There were times I wanted to throw the computer out the window. Were all the headaches worth it? Absolutely! In the process, God always shows up and showcases His faithfulness taking a manuscript mess and turning it into a message.

I will continue to live my dream of being an author, but the credit will always go to the One who pushes my pen forward. What dreams are you waiting to fulfill? It may seem impossible at first, but God can get you there if you are using your gifts to honor Him.

REFLECTION:

Day 22...Evening

DREAMS DO COME TRUE

"Be joyful in hope, patient in affliction, faithful in prayer." Romans 12:12

Delighted to say that becoming a published author was a dream. Not one that I was conscious of at first as the road that got me there was life altering. You may have heard this a time or two before, but out of hard times comes something good.

Reflecting over the years, I see how each piece, each season, got me to where I am today. Once that dream was revealed to me and I persevered it became a reality. Which in turn inspired me to dream bigger. And that I did! Currently, I have four books published and available to readers. As well as a writing group collaboration that produced two books. A few articles and poems were published along this journey, and I am working on some new releases in this season. I have learned that the dream was about offering hope to those feeling hopeless and unsure in life. Many moments dreaming and many more moments watching it all play out blessed my heart and built within me the desire to help others heal, feel and do.

So many are idle, wanting to do it, yet not sure where to start. Or others are so busy with the demands of life that dreams, passions, and creativity get left behind. Scripture tells us to use the gifts the Lord has given us and to share those gifts with others.

There is another dream being revealed at this time. I am excited to see it bloom. With prayer, heart and putting one foot in front of the other I know that dream too will come true.

How about you? What dreams are you working towards? Or what dreams do you hold in your heart, but have not put in motion? Take time today and ask God to open the doors. If He does, then go ahead and put one foot in front of the other and get to stepping. Dreams do come true and there is a dream with your name on it.

REFLECTION:

Day 23...Morning

INSPIRATIONAL SPACES

Let the heavens be glad and let the earth rejoice; let the sea roar, and all that fills it. Psalm 96:11

Living along the coastline offers many little spots to stop and be inspired. One such space for me is to drive along A1A with music playing and either the windows down or sunroof open. Fresh air, tunes, blue skies or a starry night just fills my soul.

Along the way to A1A is the causeway. As I drive over it, I like to pull off and sit at a picnic table under the trees. The river flows, birds fly, and fish leap in the tide. It's a beautiful sight and words come to my mind so easily when I visit these majestic spaces.

Poems, short stories and words of encouragement have been the results of my random drives. When the desire tugs at my soul, I get up and go. Countless times and yet, I am often inspired as it never seems to get old. Creation at its best right before my eyes leaves my mind in awe.

God has given us much beauty in His creation. It's all around regardless of where we might live. Sometimes it is visible and sometimes it requires us to simply take it all in and let that be a time of revealing. Take a scroll through social media for just a few moments and I can pretty much guarantee you will see some posts of amazing places people have been to. The good news is we don't have to go far to witness these incredible spaces because they are available to us all.

Perhaps today as you walk, drive, bike, however it is you may move, let the beauty that surrounds you also inspire you. When you are still, find a window or a patio, a chair and take the time to look and to see. Rest assured beauty will find you and so will inspiration. They go hand in hand.

REFLECTION:

Day 23...Evening

INSPIRATIONAL SPACES

He has made everything beautiful in its time. He has also set eternity in the human heart; yet no one can fathom what God has done from beginning to end. Ecclesiastes 3:11

There are places that feel like home away from home. A space where you can feel right and joy abounds. It can be somewhere you get to really let your hair down and relax. It's a place where your heart finds peace and fulfillment. Someone else may walk in it and not feel the same emotional pull you do. It's personal in every way.

The last time I was in Louisiana, I didn't want to leave. The newest member of my family lives there and this grandma is madly in love with him. I know vacation is different than living everyday there, but I long for the Southern hospitality of "yes ma'am, no sir," and holding doors open. The spread of land and homes with large porches where you drink iced tea on a star filled night. Hands raised high by faded jeans and cowboy hats wearing folks, with big hearts on fire for Christ, and family.

In my own state there is a place I love to visit. It's a small town on the East Coast, tucked away between busy cities. Time stood still in this lovely nostalgic place. It has rolling hills and vintage lanterns on the street corners and small shops. It is easy to imagine a horse and carriage strolling through those narrow, cobblestone streets instead of modern cars. When the sun kisses the ocean signaling the end of the day, God paints a beautiful display of pinks and purples across the quiet sky. Birds soar freely into the illuminated canvas. In that moment, the magnitude of God's handiwork leaves me in awe.

Both places are very different, but they both covey peace and relaxation. God dwells in places I have been to and will dwell in places I have yet to go.

What kind of places inspire you? Wherever they are, God is with you there.

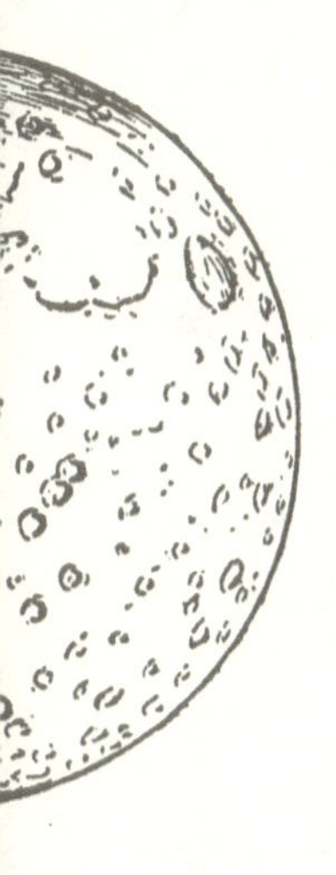

REFLECTION:

Day 24...Morning

GOOD INFLUENCE

For He chose us in Him before the creation of the world to be holy and blameless in his sight. Ephesians: 1:4

It wasn't a two-way conversation. It was the weight of words written on a piece of paper given to me by a stranger as I waited for a bus. These were unspoken words that would start a conversation that would change who I was.

Through the years our self-esteem can get bruised and trampled. Betrayal and hurt mars the image you see in the mirror every day. It takes the right kind of guidance to heal all those wounds.

When I read those words on my commute that day, a conversation began in my mind. It traveled to my soul and resided there for a few years. From time to time, I would think about the words, but they lay dormant, covered up by my unforgiveness and hurt. Occasionally, I would pull out that tract wanting to believe what I was reading, but it brought up questions that hung in the silence like a heavy load I was forced to carry.

That message on that paper became a pivotal part of a conversation years later. This time I was encouraged to check out the Bible for the answers. What I found was I didn't need to change my looks or be someone's emotional punching bag. I could genuinely be myself. The answers to all my questions had a name and He had written a love letter to me with His own blood on Calvary. Jesus loved us so much He died to save the whole world. That included me! As imperfect as I was, He loved me!The tract, the questions, the conversations weren't a bunch of random coincidences, as some may think. These were influenced by God who wanted me to know who I was and whom I belonged to.

I have given out that same gospel track to others, in hope that it would start a conversation inside their souls. That this simple act could influence them to seek Jesus. Then they would know beyond a shadow of a doubt, they were loved too! Do you know how much He loves you?

REFLECTION:

Day 24...Evening

GOOD INFLUENCE

Whoever walks with the wise becomes wise, but the companion of fools will suffer harm. Proverbs 13:20

I have been fortunate to have had great conversations across my years. Some difficult ones as well. Usually, I listen and offer encouragement. It comes naturally and since I tell it straight there is no room for misunderstanding. Or at least I like to think so.

Reflecting on a conversation that made a positive impact on me even though I resisted the messenger. What does that mean? Well, I was unwilling to receive what was said. Feelings of agitation surfaced. "You are called to lead ladies ministry." Laughter was my response. Honestly, right at the pastor as he said it. Shook my head, "No, not me." As a small business owner with many daily tasks, I did not have time to sit around sipping tea and eating cookies in ministry. He in return laughed back at me.

An in-depth conversation produced fruit, as I stood at a podium addressing a group. Yes, you guessed right. I became the ministry leader, fell into that role not with resentment or obligation, but with passion. Beautiful experiences and tough ones too, far too many to share now. However, without regret and with great admiration for that initial conversation.

Sixteen years later, I laugh again as I know what I resisted has been exactly what I was called to do. It's the plan, in my DNA to be active in the community. Perhaps not with tea and cookies, though some days with coffee and convo, and with the Word and sweet love for people. From "No, not me to Yes, me, and Yes to you too."

Learning the hard way seems to be common practice. It leads to frustration and feelings of failure. Following God's way allows for all He planned to flourish. In hindsight, we see the fruit of what His handprints were all over and the rot of what we gripped tightly to. There is a huge difference between the two and the evidence will be obvious. God has a plan for each of us. Scripture shares that we are wonderfully made and with great purpose. Take some time to sit and ponder, am I saying no to God's plan?

REFLECTION:

Day 25...Morning

IN RETROSPECT

Set your mind on things above, not on earthly things. Colossians 3:2

I can so appreciate that I have learned to trust the Lord. That my need to be in charge or in control has somehow lessened, taken a back seat and frankly, I am okay with it.

In the past, without defining a time frame, I went from being the do person to I still do, but, on a different level now. Where I use to get mad or stressed out wearing my Superwoman cape I can now chuckle, sit back and say what many take a lifetime to express, "Whatever."

Don't get me wrong, I love to set up events, start groups and rally for a cause, yet I no longer feel the need to "get er done" so to say as a one-person team. What is that quote? "There is no I in team." I'd rather be involved without the responsibility of running the show.

Now after years of doing, picking up the slack and calling the shots I can show true appreciation for that quote. As well as stepping back, sometimes even stepping out and watching others get invested and then together as a team we do.

I have come a long way with still more to work on. Thus far, I appreciate every lesson and every moment I have walked through.

How about you? Are you the take charge person or the run the other way person? The Word says we are one body with many parts. The world says too many cooks in the kitchen spoil the soup. I honestly have tried to be the whole body and have tasted the soured soup. In retrospect, yes in looking back, I have come to find being a part of the body and filling a spot on the team makes great food for the soul.

REFLECTION:

Day 25...Evening

IN RETROSPECT

My sheep hear my voice, and I know them, and they follow me...John 10:27-28

When I was a little girl, I didn't appreciate the quiet. Noise was something I craved. The laughter and even the bickering with siblings did not exist. As an only child, I spent a lot of time in my make-believe world. A place where I had a very large family. My pretend family was extremely vocal, filled with opinions and distinctive personalities. That must be where my love of dialogue in my writing comes from.

There are times when I still need to fill my space with noise. Those are times anxiety rears its ugly head and being alone with my own thoughts is not a good idea. These intrusive thoughts create unhelpful chatter. As a believer in Christ, I know that hearing faith-building words will set my heart back to its normal rhythm and my mind to its balanced state. To accomplish this, I need to be intentional with what noise I let in. The noise that works best is the sound of worship music or a faith building sermon. Even scrolling through the media pages of Christian speakers who inspire or encourage my soul, changes the negative commentary.

The enemy has many tactics to distract us from the voice of God. It feeds our egos and traps us with its empty promises. When he can't get us through flattery, he uses guilt. Do you recognize the loop? It says, you are a failure, you aren't good enough, you don't matter. God's voice says the opposite, you are an overcomer, you are forgiven, you are loved. We can distinguish God's voice because it always brings conviction but not condemnation. His voice is the voice of healing and restoration.

When my soul is at peace, the quiet is more inviting. It is a perfect time for journaling or starting a new writing project. The calm of the night is also a good time to reflect on my day and thank God for all the good in my life. It's the time I can truly appreciate the beauty of silence, because in that silence God speaks.

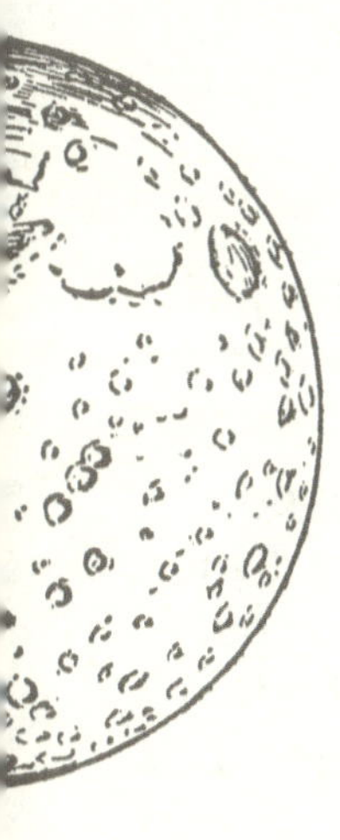

REFLECTION:

Day 26...Morning

GRATITUDE

Give thanks in all circumstances; for this is God's will for you in Christ Jesus. 1 Thessalonians 5:18

There are so many things we can be thankful for every day of our lives. Little things like the smell of freshly cut grass, or the sunlight that seeps through the windowpane. Or big things like figuring out where a manuscript page went, because you were sure you had saved it on your desktop. Glitches are not part of my personal thank you list, however, having a computer is!

My gratitude list may lack thankfulness for glitches, but it cheers for the technology to see my little grandbaby on video chat. Thanks to this modern marvel, even though he had not seen me since he was born, he threw his arms out and cooed that he wanted to be held by his "Abuela." This had me smiling from ear to ear!

There are little things that barely show up in our thankfulness scale. The irony is these things are vital for survival. When I pour myself a cup of icy water, I don't automatically stop to think that drinking water cold or not, is a luxury in other countries like Africa and Cuba. It only becomes part of my prayer list when the mechanism on the dispenser stops working. Then it hits the top of my thankfulness list when it gets fixed. How many things do we forget to be thankful for until we don't' have them any longer?

Pain, and all kinds of interesting symptoms that stem from my Fibromyalgia diagnosis. Bad flare ups can come without a warning. Yet, I have found ways to write, travel, drive, and enjoy my life. Others my same disorder have symptoms 24/7 that make it impossible to function without assistance. For me days without severe pain are a God sent!

A heart of gratitude starts with the right perspective. We can gripe about what we don't have, or we can look a little closer and see how many blessings we have been given! What are you thankful for today?

REFLECTION:

Day 26...Evening

GRATITUDE

Be thankful in all circumstances, for this is God's will for you who belong to Christ Jesus. 1 Thessalonians 5:18

When we hear words like thankful and grateful our ears usually pay attention. Those words reflect something appreciated and can be used universally. Being in appreciation for people, an opportunity, or an outcome, sets a tone for us to really grasp just how blessed we are for the big and small occurrences throughout our lives. All too often these blessings are taken for granted as a perk or part of everyday life.

I like to walk in the realm of daily blessings and take notes of the miracles that happen. Walking in faith and trusting without sight presents numerous moments of praising God. Without Him, nothing is possible, yet, with Him everything is possible. Honestly, that gets overlooked far too much in the busy lives of us believers. I say this not to condemn anyone, but to simply get us to look around. Each day there is an opportunity to be thankful and full of gratitude. God is gracious in every moment.

So, let's take this moment now, what are you thankful for? Can you list three things?

For me, I am most grateful for the opportunity to be present, to see, hear, and feel. Secondly, time – to sit at the kitchen table while my daughter is coloring, her hands are steady, her color choices smooth and realistic. Our conversation is flowing. I love the relationship we have built from hanging out watching a show, to making a meal to deeper topics of life. And finally, I am ever so grateful for the sound of keys in the door announcing my husband is home and safe. His voice, "Hello." fills my heart and puts a smile on my face.

So basically, I am grateful for my family and the time I get to share with them. There are so many moments to be grateful for, my mind, my heart and my mouth give praise in all circumstances.

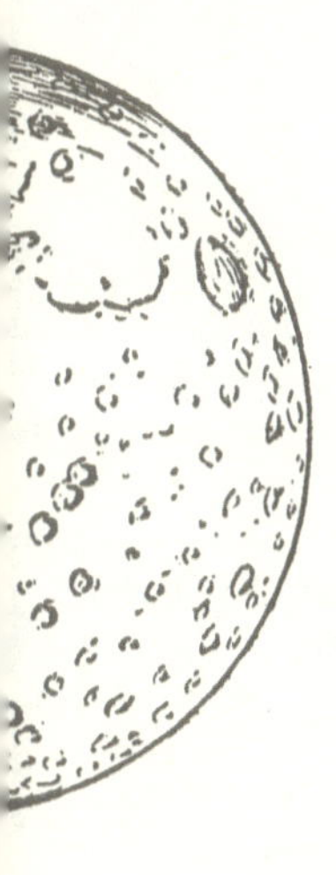

REFLECTION:

Day 27...Morning

NEWSFLASH

Whoever speaks the truth gives honest evidence, but a false witness utters deceit. Proverbs 12:17

Not to get self-righteous or political, but so much of what we see on the news, in print and on social media is distorting the truth. Sometimes it's total fabrication, more times than not it creates negative consequences. Battles over world situations can get downright ugly. I personally try to be unbiased and I know how I respond to anything is on me.

So now that I opened that can of worms, I will use the ways of the world we are living as the canvas for awareness and reaction. Situations, past and present, affect us all. Differences of opinions across the globe will be heard and as we have witnessed can cause some deep-rooted anger and hatred.

Life seems to be full speed ahead into chaos. A blatant disregard for human life is certainly elevated. It's not a new thing, yet it points to a godless society. Despite the chaotic under tone there is much goodness still visible in today's world. Perhaps that made you laugh, but it is true. Again, awareness and reaction are key elements to how we live.

Scripture provides stories of people who have been positive and negative in words, thoughts and actions. We read about horrific situations that leave us feeling where is justice? God is a Lord of justice. He will judge the righteous and yes, the wicked too. That is our news flash to remember.

Flapping our tongues declaring to be heard are instinct. Stopping our fingers from commenting on post are a learned practice. I say this, always stand up for your faith as is told in scripture. However, getting into the daily toxicity is not honoring God. Where your focus is, your mind will follow! Today's news flash, God's got it and God wins!

REFLECTION:

Day 27...Evening

NEWSFLASH

And we know that for those who love God all things work together for good, for those who are called according to his purpose. Romans 8:28

There is always bad news playing daily on every social media outlet. Most of the time, the good news gets buried under it. Yet, inspiring stories continue to happen every day, even if they aren't all broadcast.

There is a survival story that touched my heart when it aired. After a flash flood that claimed the lives of many innocent people in Texas, one courageous voice stood out from the rising waters. The viewers were told how singing praises to the Lord had kept her calm as the waters rose. The modern-day survivor, rewrote a popular song telling her survival story. The faith filled words echoed a message of hope to many grieving families. It served as a light that pierced the darkness of that day. Out of something so tragic, this survivor brought the attention back to the saving blood of Jesus.

This modern-day story echoes a story from the Bible where Paul and Silas had been beaten and were thrown in jail for preaching about Jesus. These men prayed and worship the Lord in song while incarcerated. As a result, the doors of the prison flung open, and they were escorted out by the jailer who also became a believer, Acts 16:16-40.

We all have stories. They may not appear in the headlines, but they are just as important. God allows us to have experiences that highlight His involvement in our lives. Through them, we can find healing and help others heal as well. If you look at what you experienced through the lens of "God is a good God no matter what," you will see His hand. It's the same hand that made it possible for you to be here at this precise moment, reading this devotional.

REFLECTION:

Day 28...Morning

SUMMERTIME BLISS

The heart of man plans his way, but the Lord establishes his steps. Proverbs 16:9

As a child summer days were filled with yummy, cherry-flavored, popsicle juice running down my chin. Sounds of laughter as I played tag with my cousins permeated the warm air. Those were carefree summers, void of adult responsibilities.

Once I became a teenager, summer meant working at a posh boutique and saving up to buy fashionable clothing. In the 80's my summer nights were spent cruising Miami Beach with my friends. Windows down, song blaring through the speakers, as we searched the streets for our knight in shining shorts and flip flops.

As a grown adult, the summer of 2025 came without fanfare. There was no postcard sun-kissed vacations on the horizon. It was the summer of medical appointments and diagnostic tests. However, in the middle of all that, we were invited to attend our grandbaby's dedication. We would have to factor in some health challenges to make the trip, but we didn't want to miss it. God answered our prayers when my son and his girlfriend volunteered to drive.

Normally when we travel to my daughter's we stay in a hotel. We have our favorite that is not too far from where she lives. We are on first name basis with the server at the small café down the street. This is time, my daughter had booked for her family and ours a rugged, spacious, Airbnb. I admit, I was not pleased at first with the accommodation. Yet to my surprise, we spent four glorious days enjoying precious baby coos, eating home cooked meals, and relaxing. After my grandbaby's dedication at the church, everyone brought dishes to share, and we ended the night playing board games as new friendships were formed.

Summer bliss happens when we let go of what we think ought to be, and we trust God with what is.

REFLECTION:

Day 28...Evening

SUMMERTIME BLISS

"For everything there is a season, and a time for every matter under heaven." Ecclesiastes 3:1

Time, how I truly enjoyed making quality time with my husband and family, to indulge in moments like walks, exercise, cooking new meals and taking day trips. Winging it so to say. Whether it's a short drive or an adventure did not matter. What did matter though is the choice to do it and then following through.

Someday and when we can afford it would no longer suffice. So we pulled out the calendar and planned, nothing fancy, but we did it. Visits to historic landmarks, museums, concerts, art shows, car shows, wineries, distilleries, zoos and botanical gardens. Along with pop-ins to see loved ones. We were so-called gypsies and loved it. The hubby and I have truly spoiled ourselves this past summer more than ever before.

However, the best thing about summer was coming home. Walking in the door, getting pup love and sitting out back with family, neighbors, food and conversation. Blessed to the extreme! Home sweet home.

I recall reading about the prodigal son. He longed for home and walked in that direction, his father ran to embrace him. I don't know if that was a summer day or not, but I trust it became a favorite day, one to remember and cherish. How about you? Is there a time that filled you with bliss?

God blesses us daily. We may not always recognize the blessing, but it is there none the less. Take a moment to reflect on your day, week, month, and year and then thank Him for the bliss.

REFLECTION:

Day 29...Morning

A MOMENT IN TIME

Come to me all who are weary, and I will give you rest.
Matthew 11:28

This month went by so fast! Like the blink of an eye and it is gone. For me, it was productive as a few doors opened and I jumped right in. Exciting yet demanding, which required a lot of my time, often leaving little time for self-care.

I have learned the hard way, as I am sure many of you have too, that putting yourself last will not result in anything good. So, with a new month only hours away, I do look forward to doing what is necessary, but also to slowing down. How can that happen?

First, I must admit to myself that things are going too fast and I need rest. For me, known as the energizer bunny, that is hard, regardless, rest is necessary. Second, after declaring it, I must follow that with action. Yes, action, not in continuing in the same manner. Instead, take action to slow down. It can be done and I will do it. Why?

Simply put, because I need to and God commands it. Jesus tells us to come, and we will find rest in Him. Scripture is not just pretty words, it's a promise. These words are for me, yet also for you. Are you taking time for self-care, time to simply rest?

Why is it that we go and go until we fall? Our minds convince us that we must. However, God does for us, he makes the way and provides our needs. Is it enough, do we need more? Seems our actions say yes to that question as we continue to press on the endless cycle of go and do.

Think on this, even Jesus took time for himself. He went to be alone, to pray and to be with the Father. If we are to live in His image, then taking time for yourself should be a normal part of our lives. Resting in His presence allows us to be refreshed. Once we are, we can go out and be where we are meant to be. Let's stop making it hard on ourselves and get to resting. He is waiting with open arms.

REFLECTION:

Day 29...Evening

A MOMENT IN TIME

...weeping may stay for the night, but rejoicing comes in the morning. Psalm 30:5

Some moments remain etched in our minds for as long as we are alive. My mother's last day on earth is one of those moments. The memories still bring tears, but because my mom was a believer when she went, I did not grieve without hope.

The last days of her life, Hospice nurses were dispatched to our home The evening nurse was a sweet lady who hummed Christian hymns as she took care of my mom who was in coma. The night before she passed, the nurse assured me that she would wake me up if the vitals showed my mom was starting her transition. Exhausted from days of apprehensive tension, I fell asleep.

Early that morning she woke us up. We all went to my mother's bedside in our pajamas. There we were, my two kids, my father, and my husband. We knew church was going on. It was a sunny Sunday morning, and my heart was breaking into a thousand pieces.

We had church right there next to my mom. If anyone saw us, they would have assumed that we were in denial or we had lost our mind. An unexplainable peace flowed into the room when I opened the scriptures and read. There was a comforting blend of sorrow and joy when our cracked voices sang praises to our Lord. Odd enough, the tears in my eyes were not flowing as one would expect, even though my heart was being crushed with each shallow breath she took.

Her transition was very slow. Hospice explained that sometimes loved ones try to hold on longer because they are worried about leaving their family behind. I was told that I needed to give her permission to go be with Jesus. I still don't know how I mustered the courage to mouth the painful words that assured her that it was okay to leave, but I did. She went peacefully into eternity.
In moments of wrecking pain, God takes over. He wraps us in His arms when we need Him and turns our weeping into rejoicing.

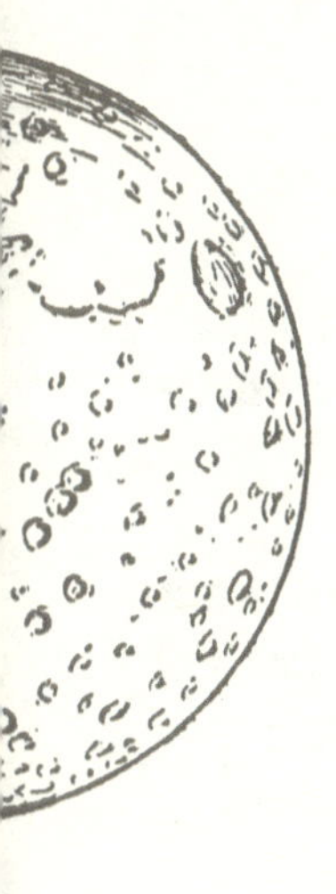

REFLECTION:

Day 30...Morning

LOOKING FORWARD

"Satisfy us in the morning with your unfailing love, that we may sing for joy and be glad all our days". Psalm 90:14

Cubans have a little tradition that we follow every 31st of December. We eat 12 grapes at the stroke of midnight, one for each month. If the grape you eat is sweet, you will have a great month. If it is sour, well, it will be a month full of trouble. It may be a fun tradition, but God is the only one who determines our days. We can't predict how a year will turn out. However, we can look forward to God's blessing every month. We can be hopeful and find comfort in Him when the calendar does not look promising.

This January I was forced to take a hiatus from my writing. My personal life had interrupted the flow of creativity. Ideas for a book had surfaced but quickly died as I struggled to balance multiple caregiving responsibilities. The inspirational words that kept me grounded in the colder months were slipping away like melting snow. By May I felt like I was drowning in the torrential rainstorm of round-the-clock care for my loved ones. The scorching Florida heat in June through September singed the edges of my resilience. Overwhelmed by the emotional toll and loneliness. That trying month seemed to never end. Then when I thought the year had been a complete flop, God answered. My tears became cathartic, they ushered in acceptance and grace.

Between pumpkin lattes and fall leaves decorations, God continued to infuse me with His peace, allowing inspiration to fly in on the wings of the cooler breeze. Freed from the clutches of resentment, my renewed creativity filled the pages of written material.

I am excited to see what opportunities will mark my calendar going forth. I can't wait to see His plan unfold. I don't know what this season looks like for you right now. It may be filled with overflowing joy, or it may keep you on your knees. Either way God has a purpose for all your seasons. He can bless and restore or reconstruct and realign. He can meet you in the middle of your greatest challenge and turn all your sour grapes into a sweet tasting treat.

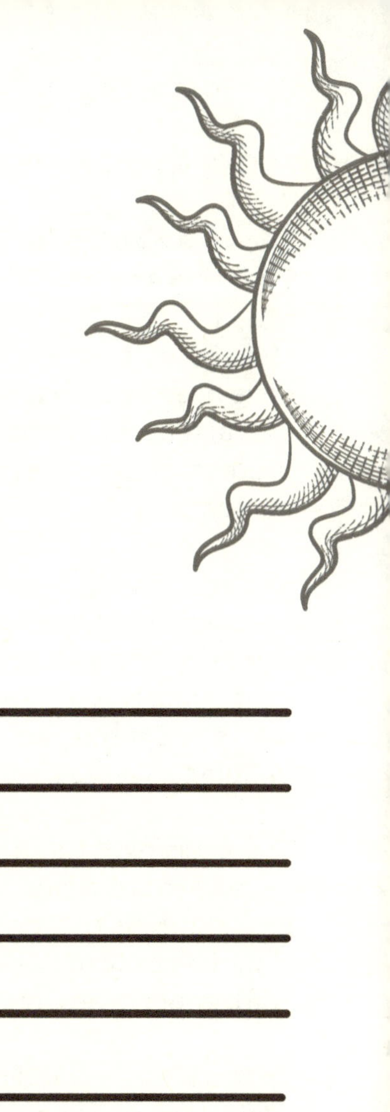

REFLECTION:

Day 30...Evening

LOOKING FORWARD

"I can do all this through him who gives me strength."
Philippians 4:13

Most of us, if honest, dwell on the past. We are looking at where we have been and what we have experienced. Truly it keeps us distracted, yet I know we can learn from things in our past. The problem is when we get stuck there or discouraged because of the outcomes.

Moving forward is encouraged in our daily lives. Scripture tells us to keep our eyes fixed on Jesus because he makes the way. That takes a whole lot of pressure off us, don't you think? So why is it that we continuously look at what is done? Then, when we do look forward, we try to set the pace. We make a list of things to do, places to go, people to see, as if we are in control.

There it is right there, control. I recognize it because I admittingly have been there and for far too long! With seasons of life that brought trials to face, uncertainties at every corner, discouragement would be easy to fall in to. I did, yet something inside said, "Wait." So, I did, until I heard loud and clear, "Press on."

That is where I stand today, pressing on. The course has changed again, but I have let go of taking control. Not a minute of it was easy, I grumbled each step of the way to get to the point of let go, let God. Looking forward is what my focus is on with whatever time the Lord is granting me. Trusting in his plan and surrendered to mine.

I know I can only move in his strength. My own strength failed me. Your strength will fail you as well. Not to be negative, it is in our bible. Here is a bit of encouragement, today, hand over the burdens, pride, and the need to be the front runner in all things in your life. Instead, take a seat and pray. Wait, listen and when you hear him, that will be the right time to move forward. He knows the plan; He has authored your story. If you need to look back, then glance at all the times He has been there with you and He is by your side even now.

REFLECTION:

Night

Always comes to be
After a full day
Setting up rest
Hours of busyness
Have drained these tired bones
Along inner quest

Time goes by swiftly
Filled with much to do
Day turns to night
Mind and body fade
Begging for refuel
God's Word – makes it right

Author Kim Doran

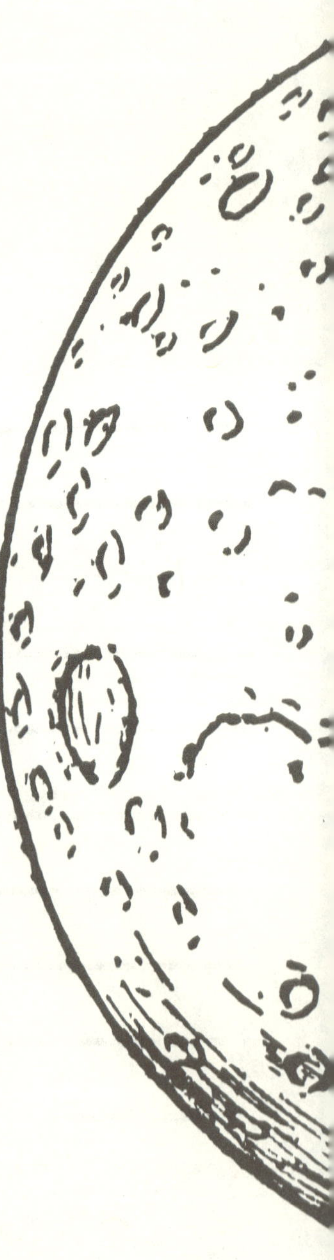

Thank you first and foremost to God.

Thank you to our families and friends who have supported us every step of the way.

Also, if you are reading this...

Thank you!

Ileana Leon

Ileana M. Leon is an author dedicated to leaving readers with a renewed sense of hope. Through both fiction and non-fiction, she explores real-life struggles with compassion and faith.

In her romance espionage novel, On the Edge of Truth, Ileana highlights the importance of
forgiveness and trust. In her self-care book, Fear Less Living, she shares her personal journey with anxiety and equips readers with practical strategies and faith-based tools to help them face fear and find peace. Her work raises awareness, reduces stigma, and empowers others to move from victim to survivor and ultimately overcomer.

Her writing is inspired by her earlier career as a paralegal and her work for Children and Family Services. Ileana continues to be a voice for mental health awareness and special needs families, while remaining active in faith-based ministries. In her free time, she enjoys curling up with a good book or expressing her creativity through hands-on projects.

She resides in sunny Port Saint Lucie, Florida, with her family. For speaking engagements, email her at leonwrites4truth@gmail.com. Her books can be found on Amazon.

Kim Doran

Kim Doran is an author that tells it straight from the heart. As a former Private Investigator and cancer overcomer, she writes from a place of truth from both her professional and personal life. Kim uses words of hope and encouragement in her poetry and self-care books.

As an author, speaker and ministry leader Kim has seen, heard and lived many of the obstacles this world presents. However, her faith keeps her focused on moving forward and helping others by teaching self-care and writing workshops as a therapeutic tool for inner growth.

Additionally, she is a co-host of Unfiltered Talk Live, an unscripted online show that dives into topics chosen by the audience. Currently, she is working on her next poetry collection.

Kim resides in Jensen Beach, Florida with her husband, daughter and two dogs. She loves the outdoors, music, open-mic nights and cooking in her free time.

Her books are available on Amazon.com. If interested in Kim speaking at your next event, contact her at kimdoranspeaks@gmail.com. Visit www.kimdoran.com

www.ingramcontent.com/pod-product-compliance
Lightning Source LLC
LaVergne TN
LVHW091004080826
845145LV00003B/1120

* 9 7 8 1 7 3 7 1 5 6 3 2 1 *